Helen Van Pelt Wilson's
AFRICAN-VIOLET BOOK

Other books by Helen Van Pelt Wilson:

THE AFRICAN VIOLET

AFRICAN VIOLET AND GESNERIAD QUESTIONS
Answered by 20 Experts

CLIMBING ROSES

THE COMPLETE BOOK OF AFRICAN VIOLETS

THE FLOWER ARRANGEMENT CALENDAR
1947–1967

FLOWER ARRANGEMENT DESIGNS FOR TODAY

A GARDEN IN THE HOUSE

THE GARDENER'S BOOK OF VERSE
Poems for Five Seasons

GERANIUMS-PELARGONIUMS

THE JOY OF FLOWER ARRANGING

THE JOY OF GERANIUMS

THE NEW PERENNIALS PREFERRED

1001 AFRICAN VIOLET QUESTIONS ANSWERED

PERENNIALS PREFERRED

THE FRAGRANT YEAR
(with Léonie Bell)

HOUSEPLANTS FOR EVERY WINDOW
(with Dorothy H. Jenkins)

ROSES FOR PLEASURE
(with Richard Thomson)

Helen Van Pelt Wilson's

African-Violet Book

by
Helen Van Pelt Wilson

HAWTHORN BOOKS, INC.
Publishers
New York

To all those
Enthusiasts
For whom their African-violets
Are not just plants but a way of life

WITH GRATITUDE

More than twenty-five years ago the *Ladies' Home Journal* in Philadelphia, much to their surprise, found themselves deluged with requests for a pamphlet they had offered on African-violets. When I wrote this, there were only about a dozen named varieties and I thought the plant was practically unknown. Not so. Many houseplant enthusiasts were trying it out and many were pleased with its continuous bloom. Others were frustrated but persistent. Anyway it was all pretty hit or miss as to culture and when new varieties were offered, confusion reigned.

Furthermore, only a few firms offered saintpaulias along with their other plants. Among them were Anne and Frank Tinari of Huntingdon Valley, Pa. They "came to violets" as a specialty, giving up their other plants in 1945. Twenty-five varieties were listed on their first postcard. Anne and Frank have been dear friends and mentors since my early days with African-violets. Like the rest of us, they learned as they grew, and business was so flourishing that on Sundays even small Frank helped with the customers. He's married now with a child of his own, and his brother Tony, born after the first saintpaulia excitement, is now in high school. The daughters, Lilianne and Clementine, and grandchildren live close by. To add to the Tinaris' happiness and honors, Frank Sr., in 1969, was elected president of the African Violet Society of America. The Tinaris have always helped with plants and advice whenever I have been writing about African-violets, and on this big revision I am again most grateful to them.

In time I also came to know Ruth and Lyndon Lyon of Dolgeville, N.Y. They started with that dangerous concept, "only a hobby," but the mutations of their first plants proved irresistible and today they are famous for their fine hybrids, including many miniatures. Lyndon writes "We are also hot on the trail of a new family of real trailers, miniatures, and others, in the full range of color and flower types." Like the Tinari family, the Lyon children got into the act and, if you stop at one of their greenhouses, you will probably see even the grandchildren helping out. Again I am grateful to Lyndon for the beautiful miniature plants he sent me, for his pictures, and also for answering my many questions on hybridizing.

In Linwood, N.J., the Fischers, father and son, and hopefully in time the new grandson, form another family business. They are presently working with the free-blooming German Rhapsodie varieties that will undoubtedly make the saintpaulia popular in the florist business. Covered with blooms, like my deep purple 'Ruth' for one, these plants shine out in any retail display. I am most grateful to Dr. Charles W. Fischer, Jr. for the fine collection he gave me to try.

As always in my saintpaulia endeavors, Alma Wright (Mrs. Robert O. Wright), has been friend and counsellor, guiding me to many sources of information, reading much of the new text, and making available from her magazine, *Gesneriad Saintpaulia News,* a number of the new illustrations that appear in this revision. Her son, Bob, whom we knew as a boy at our conventions, is grown up now and the expert photographer of the handsome GSN pictures in color. My friendship with Alma also goes back to the early days, and I am grateful for that as well as for her indefatigable assistance with this book.

Many others have contributed in one way or another and deserve my heartfelt thanks:

Christos C. Mpelkas and E. D. Bickford of Sylvania Lighting Products in Danvers, Mass.; Rufus C. Neas of Neas Growers Supply Co. of Greenville, S. C.; and Douglas Hill and John K. Michel of Duro-Lite Lamps, Inc. in Fair Lawn, N. J., for their careful checking of the statements on the growth lights now so important in saintpaulia culture.

Bernard C. Greeson, of Milwaukee, Wis., who is a fountain of knowledge on the pests and diseases we must sometimes cope with. He has performed the inestimable service to amateurs of selling soil additives and spray materials in *small* quantities. The Quick Reference Trouble Chart is his work.

Dr. Sheldon C. Reed of St. Paul, Minn., for checking once more the chapter on hybridizing. He assures me that my dicussion of genetics is still sound but tells me that mutations in saintpaulias are less frequent now than fifteen years ago.

Professor Herbert Streu of Rutgers University for information on nematodes. His investigation was supported by the Boyce Edens Research Fund of the African Violet Society of America.

Toru Arisumi of the U.S. Department of Agriculture for his advice on various species of saintpaulia and certain hybrids of S. shumensis, information resulting from a first-hand study of these plants in connection with a research project of the U.S.D.A.

Léonie Bell of Conshohocken, Pa., for her beautiful plant portraits, some of which are now on permanent exhibit at The Hunt Botanical Library in Pittsburg.

Kathleen Bourke of Kathleen Bourke Associates of Kansas City, Mo., for the skillful how-to drawings whose clarity is the result of experience, for she too grows African-violets.

Lucile C. Rainsberger of Lambertville, Mich., whose knowledge is both wide and deep (she doubts if she has "over 3,000 plants") for permitting me to include her famous Nature's Way soil formula and the account of her experience in growing show specimens under fluorescent lights.

Grace Foote, Editor of the African Violet Magazine, Helen Van Zele, Mrs. Wayne W. Schroeder and Gus Becker for making available to me illustrations from that magazine.

Ruth Katzenberger of Long Island, N.Y., the "inventor" of the enchanting miniature Sinningia 'Baby Doll' and the X Gloxinera 'Cupid's Doll', for generously sharing with me her considerable information on gesneriads in general, miniatures in particular, and culture under lights. Her husband, Alfred, designed the light cart and tells how you can make it yourself.

Daniel T. Walden for his infinite editorial patience and meticulous copy-editing of my manuscript.

Finally, Helen B. Krieg, not only for her superior typing but also for her unfailing good humor and optimistic faith that this revision really would be completed—and here it is!

H. V. P. W.
Westport, Conn.

CONTENTS

LIST OF ILLUSTRATIONS

Color Illustrations

Helen Van Pelt Wilson's
AFRICAN-VIOLET BOOK

Helen Van Pelt Wilson's Plant Room, facing south and west, is filled with African-violets; one of her fluorescent lights is seen above the casements. Bradbury photo.

1

ALWAYS IN BLOOM

The Amen! of Nature is always a flower.
Oliver Wendell Holmes

Flowers, that's what we grow African-violets for, and we want flowers all the time, not just now and then. What's more, we can have them almost continuously at our windows or under fluorescent lights. It's all a matter of knowing how to treat the plants and then giving them *regular* attention. African-violets are really very amenable. They even prefer it nice and warm the way we do, not the chilly temperature many other houseplants prefer. Furthermore, the newer cultivars are likely to be far more floriferous than earlier varieties.

However, there are saintpaulia admirers who claim it is "a stubborn plant." Yet difficulties apparently do not affect popularity. Hundreds of varieties are now eagerly sought by thousands of fanciers, many of whom repeatedly ask, "How can I make them bloom?" Experts at flower shows are asked this question over and over again. For every enthusiast who claims, "My plants are practically never out of bloom," there are many who have not yet learned the "trick," and can only lament, "Lots of leaves but almost no buds!"

TRUTH ABOUT FLOWERING

Actually, flowering is not dependent on some trick or magic formula but is the result of a number of factors that add up to good health for African-violets—and hence bloom. Even successful commercial growers do not entirely agree on culture. Despite the somewhat contradictory advice you may read or hear, certain methods of saintpaulia culture have proved satisfactory enough for many people to

1

recommend. As you consider these, keep in mind that you should have different expectations of bloom for different varieties. A realistic approach means much less disappointment.

Some of the smaller types are very free-flowering, "always in bloom." The recent German introductions, the Rhapsodies, are of this type—strong-growing as well as floriferous, much admired by an increasing number of experts, and probably a promising contribution to breeders. Many of my own Rhapsodies tended to multiple crowns with heavy bloom—fine for display. Other types, especially the Supremes, give larger but fewer flowers; or a brilliant display followed by a period of little or no bloom. Young plants obviously will not put on the show of large mature specimens. A rest period between heavy bloom is also normal for most plants, but for saintpaulias resting

In the author's study, plant trays of pebbles promote humidity. *Home Garden,* Gottscho-Schleisner photo.

This collector makes use of every possible inch of window space and grows most of the plants in square wick pots. Genereux photo.

should be a matter of days or weeks at the most, not of months. However, plants moved from greenhouse to living room might sulk that long, since your average conditions may be a far cry from the ideal ones they have been enjoying. And any variety may be a shy bloomer if not well looked after.

LIGHT, THE FIRST CONSIDERATION

Give your African-violets all the light—and as much sunshine—*as they will stand:* not full sun all day in summer, but several hours of sun in winter, especially during the morning. Sunshine produces flowers, but too much affects foliage adversely, turning it yellow, burning the margin of leaves, and causing malformation of leaf and flower. Seek the happy medium. I believe we have often been too chary of sunshine. Beautiful dark green foliage and no flowers usually are an indication of too little light.

African-violets may be grown at any window in your house that is well lighted, not darkened by trees, and at any sunny window, where the brightness is somewhat diffused or where plants can be set back a little from the sun. If you wish to use south windows, temper the brilliance of late spring and summer there with a thin curtain, a Venetian blind (keep the slats tilted upward during sunniest hours), or a screen formed by a sun-loving vine. In the short days of winter, an uncurtained south window may not be too bright. Let your African-violets tell you what light they want. In a week you can read the answer "too much sunshine" in off-color leaves.

Electrical engineers, rather than horticulturists, have used foot-candle meters to determine just how much light plants need for maximum growth and bloom. A footcandle is a unit of illumination (see Chapter 4). The number of window-sill footcandles varies from 200 or less (northern exposure on a winter day) to 8,000 or more (southern exposure in mid-June). Without measuring, we know that the stronger the light plants can *safely endure,* the deeper the color tones and the greater the number of flowers.

Be sure to keep turning your plants so that all growing parts will receive an equal amount of light. A quarter turn, clockwise, once a week is fine, but oftener if you are growing show plants.

While the saintpaulia is cultivated primarily for its flowers, foliage is also important. The amount of light is vital here, too. Spooned leaves may lose this trait when given too much light. Strong light and slightly lower temperatures will bring out reddish reverses on the leaves of certain varieties. And insufficient light may be a factor in causing the leaves of a variegated plant to turn plain green.

Indoor gardens with fluorescent illumination can be filled with perfectly symmetrical African-violets that bloom and bloom. In fact, results may be better than under greenhouse culture. Put up fluorescent fixtures in any room of your house, even in the cellar—wherever winter temperatures won't go below 60 degrees F. (For a more complete discussion of culture under fluorescent lights, see Chapters 4 and 5.)

TEMPERATURE

Despite the 40- to 80-degree F. tolerance of their ancestors, modern saintpaulias are no more likely to thrive under the conditions their pioneer forefathers endured than we are likely to enjoy the Pilgrims' freezing hardship. In the house, African-violets like it fairly warm, a day temperature even up to 75 degrees F., but 70 to 72 degrees, is better. Their liking for heat is another good reason for popularity. Too many lovely houseplants prefer 60 degrees, and what human being is comfortable at that!

A 5-degree drop after dark, as in nature, may be desirable if your thermostat and the comfort of your home life permit. However, I think this adjustment as a need has been overemphasized. I set the thermostat in the Plant Room at 68 degrees at night; in the living room it stays where I like it at 72 degrees. The Tinaris hold night temperatures in the greenhouses at 70 degrees, especially in very cold weather. In any case, watch out for temperatures below 60 degrees. Such coolness could be an answer to non-flowering. At night in bitter weather, slip cardboard or thicknesses of newspaper between your African-violets and the window glass, or keep the shade or Venetian blind drawn. And if you have a greenhouse, watch out for extremes, especially in spring and fall. Temperatures soaring to 90 degrees in the daytime and dropping to 50 at night do not promote bloom.

A BUOYANT ATMOSPHERE

A fresh atmosphere is essential for flowering. Even in cold weather, try to avoid closeness. It's no better for plants than for you. Maintain a buoyant atmosphere. It's an inspiration to budding. Indirect ventila-

Plant stands attractively display saintpaulias. Left, Roche photo; below, Taloum-is photo.

tion from an adjoining room is the safest plan. In most dwellings where doors to the outside are frequently in use, the matter of fresh air takes care of itself.

If your African-violets are in an apartment, have a "program" of ventilation, as greenhouse men do. A good airing the first thing in the morning, and again in mid-afternoon, if you are equal to both, will promote health, and so flowering. Try closing the room where the plants are and opening a window in an adjoining room for half an hour or less, depending on weather. After you close the window, open the doors of the plant room, and the new air, not too cool now, will circulate refreshingly.

However, if gas is escaping from cookstove or heater, fresh air won't protect your plants from poisoning. Dark, almost-black, buds falling prematurely, and yellowing foliage as well as the nonflowering condition, are possible indications of gas poisoning. Gas may seep out in quantities too minute for you to notice, but enough to make your African-violets sick. If there is any possibility of this kind of trouble, why not have your gas company make an inspection? This is done free of charge.

PROPER WATERING

One factor vital to flowering is water in adequate, just-right amounts. Yet I can give you no rule as to quantity, only as to temperature. *Water must be of room temperature,* or just a little warmer. You don't have to check it with a thermometer, but take care that it is not cold, but tepid. If the water is 10 degrees above or 10 degrees below room temperature, leaf spotting may occur, even though not one drop of water touches foliage. Cold water particularly has a shocking effect, and nothing could be more of a detriment to bloom than a thorough chilling of the roots. The room-temperature rule applies also to pesticide sprays, which must be mixed with warm water, and to syringing of foliage.

Either top or bottom watering is satisfactory. I like to do both. Bottom watering is often easier for routine care. With large, spreading plants it takes more time to water carefully from the top, to hit only the soil and let no moisture run down into the crown. A long-spouted watering can is helpful for top watering. It sneaks under the close foliage, as no pitcher will ever do, but even with this, saucer watering is easier.

However, I am convinced that some top watering (and there are those who depend on it entirely) is essential to prevent accumulation

Well-grown African-violets in full bloom are moved from the window for brief display on a double white-painted hanging shelf, along with an interesting collection of china. Roche photo.

of fertilizer salts on surface of pot and soil, where they cause stem rot if petioles touch. Those salts need to be flushed down into the soil by top watering.

An excellent plan is to give the regular feeding of liquid fertilizer and the next watering from the top. Then you can do quick saucer watering the rest of the time or not, as you wish. When watering from the top, let the *feel* of the soil guide you, unless you fear you may spread mites this way. To check "by appearance of the soil" is almost impossible for such a spreading plant. Actually most of us get to know needs without much looking or feeling and have a schedule for watering, small pots every day perhaps, big ones every second or third day. Soil should never get dry, but be kept *barely* moist at all times. As it tends to dryness, pour on enough water to seep out into the saucer. This excess should be emptied after a short time. Never let your African-violets stand in water.

The *amount* of water is determined by the size and type of pot (porous or glazed), the weather (bright or dull, damp or dry), the nature of the soil, even the variety of saintpaulia. If the soil surface is still sopping wet several hours after being watered, try to pour off the excess; don't apply so much next time. If the soil surface is dry to the touch within twenty-four hours after you have watered, you haven't given enough water, or it could be that the plant has outgrown its container and needs to be repotted.

The *quality* of the water needs also to be considered—hard, soft, or full of chemicals. If you live in the Southwest, where water is strongly alkaline or hard, follow the practice of others there and water plants once a month or so with a solution of one tablespoon of vinegar to one gallon of water. If you have a water softener of the ion-exchange type, draw the water for your plants before it goes into the softener. Otherwise, the natural calcium in the water is replaced with sodium that will accumulate in the soil to the point of being toxic to plants. Once softened by this method, water is of no use to plants, as neither evaporation nor boiling will remove the sodium.

At one time a good part of houseplant ailments was blamed on purification chemicals placed in the water supplies of all municipalities. We know now that if water is safe to drink and cook with, it is perfectly all right for plants. If for any reason water becomes undrinkable, then it may be necessary to collect rainwater or melted snow, the natural and most acceptable moisture for all plants, though not if it is city rainwater or city snow, which may be badly contaminated with soot. In this predicament, you may want to rely on distilled water, available at drugstores and filling stations.

THE WICK WAY

There's nothing new about the wick method; in fact, I've had my wick pots for more than fifteen years. They are made in two parts: the upper section serves as a flowerpot, the lower, the saucer-reservoir, holds water or liquid fertilizer, and the two lock together. The wicks operate on the principle of the oil lamp, drawing water instead of oil.

Some wick pots come with a fiber-glass wicking; or you can buy fiber glass by the roll, cutting it into pieces about 1½ × 3 inches; or you can improvise with strips of nylon hose.

The attractive wick pots offer a healthful and convenient way to grow saintpaulias. They are of plastic or of clear or frosted glass, not clay, and are nicely designed—square, like my old ones, round, or oblong, and in pleasing shades of green, or all black or white, or white set in black saucers. Wick pots come in 2½- to 4¾-inch sizes; "tubs" are 4½ inches across. Larger pots are well suited to plants of considerable spread.

Wick pots make decorative accents for plants placed briefly on display on stands or tables, and they have the great advantage of being timesaving. Plants don't need going over every day; about every third day suffices for adding water. But you have to check what happens under *your* conditions. In any case, let the soil dry out just a little before refilling the reservoir. If by accident the soil gets very dry, water a little from the top after you refill the saucer. Liquid fertilizer can be applied to the top soil or poured into the reservoir. Either way seems to work. Wash the saucers with hot water about once a month. Experienced enthusiasts often use wick pots exclusively. In fact, the Robert Wrights are devoted to the wick method even unto the second generation!

Soil for wick pots needs to be light and fast draining. Alma Wright advocates a liberal amount of Sponge-Rok, perlite, or vermiculite in the mixture, also some powdered charcoal. Of course, charcoal is good in all soil mixtures, and I like to spread a little in my pebble trays to keep the water sweet there.

To prepare a wick pot for planting:

1. Unravel one end of the wick until only about 2 to 3 inches remains braided. (With some pots, wicks come unraveled for nearly an inch at both ends.)
2. Soak the wick before use; it works better when damp.
3. Pull the braided end through the large hole, which will be at the side or base of the pot.
4. Spread out the frayed end over the inside bottom of the pot and pat it flat.
5. Firmly cover the strands with a thin layer of dampened soil or peatmoss, or with a layer of drainage pebbles, and fill in with the prepared soil.

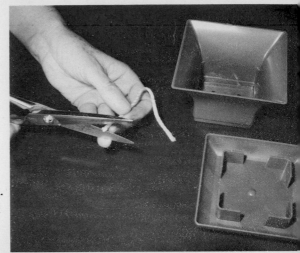

To prepare the wick, clip off the ends, if they are not already loosened so you can easily unravel them. Pull one end through the large hole in the pot.

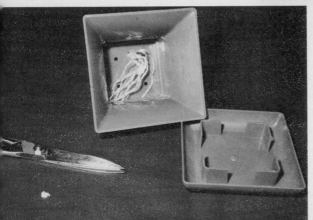

Fray the end, leaving only about 2 inches unbraided. Spread the strands over the inside bottom of the pot.

Pot as usual in a light soil mixture, allowing half-an-inch space at the top.

The wick that extends from the base of the pot will rest in the saucer and draw moisture up into the soil.

The plant is now locked into place and water is poured into the saucer reservoir. All photos from GSN.

6. Set the plant in place and work the new soil in around it, leaving about a half-inch space at the top of the pot.

7. Finally apply warm water from the top until a little drips from the exposed wick at the bottom of the pot.

8. Lock the pot into position in the saucer-reservoir and add more warm water as necessary to fill it.

At regular intervals pour liquid fertilizer into the saucer-reservoir, following the same schedule and using the same strength as for your other saintpaulias.

Wicking is a great convenience, for it can be used for automatic watering for as long as two weeks when you are away. In that case, you will want to use a longer wick, letting it reach into a quart jar or even a pail of water, the purpose being to leave an adequate two-week supply of water.

CLEANSING OF FOLIAGE

We used to think that a few drops of water on velvety saintpaulia leaves spelled doom. Now we know that nothing is more beneficial than frequent misting of foliage, provided the water used is of room temperature. Plants collect as much dust as a piano, only you are more likely to see it on the glossy wood than on a dark green leaf where it is stopping up the breathing pores of the plant. Dusty leaves are no aid to bud development.

If you live in a city where you can "never keep the house clean," better shower your African-violets at least once a month. A rubber sprayer attached to a kitchen faucet that mixes the hot and cold water to the temperature you want is fine, or you can immerse the foliage in a sink of tepid water. Your plants will revel in either treatment.

Deal with one plant at a time, hold it on its side under the spray so that the crown will escape soaking. Use your hand or a collar of polyethylene to hold soil in place. To make the plastic collar, use a 12-inch square of strong polyethylene and, halfway between two corners, make a cut to the center. Then cut out a hole 1 to 2 inches in diameter. This makes a kind of miniature barber's cloth that can be fitted neatly around the crown of an African-violet, and held around the sides of the pot while showering is underway.

In hot, dry climates frequent showering is also essential not only to cleanse but to promote humidity. Always let plants dry in a place protected from direct sunshine and drafts.

BLESSED HUMIDITY

African-violets do not thrive in a hot, dry atmosphere, and assuredly they will not bloom without plenty of humidity. If they do set buds, they will probably drop them unopened when the atmosphere is too dry. Indeed, moist air is another vital key to free flowering. African-violets like to draw in moisture from the air as well as from the soil. In many of their habitats, humidity of 60 to 70 percent prevails, so you can see how miserable they must be in a humidity of 10 to 25 percent, a not-too-uncommon winter condition in some homes and apartments. Although 60 to 70 percent may be difficult to maintain, we can usually manage 40 to 60 percent and then our African-violets will bloom well.

To measure humidity accurately, depend on an hygrometer, an instrument that I find most useful as I move it around to get readings from different locations in the house—on window sills, high-up plant shelves, pebble trays. If plants aren't thriving, the hygrometer may show the cause—too high heat, too low humidity. In the fall the early morning readings in the Plant Room may be above 62 degrees F., the humidity about the same percent. In the sunny afternoon the temperature may rise to above 70 degrees; then the humidity falls to about 40 percent. As heat goes up, relative humidity goes down, and humidity below 40 percent is not favorable to saintpaulias.

The most direct way to solve a humidity problem is to group lots of plants together. For African-violets, as well as other houseplants, I have long prized zinc trays made by a plumber to fit a series of broad window sills. The trays are an inch deep and filled with white roofing pebbles, the same kind that narcissus bulbs are grown in. The trays hold a quantity of water. The drip from top watering runs in, and I pour more, always hot, directly into the tray. Pots rest on the pebbles, *above* the level of water, which, evaporating, creates a healthful aura of humidity. This makes me extremely popular with my saintpaulias, if their blooming is any indication of affection.

If you don't want the bother of having special trays made (and today they are more expensive than when mine were made), you can use ready-made plastic trays which come in various sizes and in soft green or gray. The aluminum waterproof trays with redwood ends are attractive for a display group of African-violets.

Many find that individual African-violets thrive and bloom more freely if each plant is set on a pebble-filled saucer with some water always in it as an easy means of humidifying the surrounding air. Again, be sure the plant pots rest on the stones *above* the constant supply of water in the saucer. Damp sand may be substituted though I prefer the pebbles.

Then there are the devices called "foggers." Mine consists of a plastic bottle fitted with an atomizer top that at three feet mists so delicately that woodwork and curtains are not damaged (or at least not much!). The fogger is easily operated with one hand while the other carries the watering can. (Electric water-fog devices are also available.) Because my gadget is such fun to operate, I use it often and always between cups one and two of breakfast coffee. If you rely on such a fogger alone for humidity, better operate it about three times a day. Otherwise the dryness of the atmosphere will be hardly affected.

Central humidification is enjoyed now in many homes. It is not really a luxury, for people as well as plants find pleasantly moist air a boon to good health. In winter, a combination of 50 percent relative humidity with a 72-degree F. temperature will satisfy almost every living thing.

In a terrarium, aquarium, or battery jar, with a pane of glass placed over the opening, most pleasant and humid conditions can be constantly maintained, but it is important to keep such plantings out of the sun or they will get too hot. It is also necessary each day to raise the glass at the top and air the plants for a few minutes. Very attractive groups can be arranged for such glassed-in plantings. Particularly charming are purple African-violets, pink wax begonias, and delicate maidenhair ferns, which are likewise dependent on humidity. Only if these glass gardens are kept too wet will there be signs of decay. With so little moisture escaping, almost no watering is required. Bubble bowls, such as hold berried Christmas arrangements, are also nice for group plantings, and hardly need a glass cover. Use young rather than old plants in these arrangements since the very high humidity may be too much for mature African-violets. (More about this in Chapter 2 under Glass Containers.)

It is worth noting that older African-violets need less humidity than young ones. Too much for adults results in all sorts of troubles due to fungus, as crown, stem, and leaf rot. Young plants also seem to enjoy the ancestral temperature up to 80 degrees F., possible in covered aquariums.

One last word about supplying humidity: Don't overlook the common ways of adding moisure to the air around your violets, the steaming teakettle or electric percolator of water run in the same room, for example. Or keep a collection of decorative bottles and glasses filled with water and standing among your plants. Pans of water set on radiators help by providing a constant source of evaporation, and there are also electric vaporizers—use one supplying a cool mist, not hot steam—which have been useful, particularly in sunrooms devoted to houseplants.

WATER CULTURE IN VASES

One easy way to get quantity and size of bloom is to grow some plants the decorative way in goblets or vases of water. In winter, when cut flowers are expensive, you can have blossoms for every room by

This nicely-designed self-watering planter holds up to a thirty-day supply of plain water or a weak fertilizing solution, good for a specimen plant or a crop of leaf cuttings; a helpful device for the traveler. Acquamatic Planter photo.

growing violets this way. For a dinner party, make a lovely centerpiece by placing individual plants in jelly glasses or custard cups and grouping them in a low bowl, perhaps with pieces of ivy or philodendron inserted to create a pleasing design. I always keep rooted pieces of vines in water for this purpose.

The water-culture method for African-violets is simple enough. Select containers of a size to support crowns well above the level of the water and preferably of colored glass or pottery. Rooting seems stronger in these opaque vessels than in clear ones. Fill them three-quarters full with distilled water, fortified with Hyponex or whatever plant food you use for your earth-bound saintpaulias, and at the same strength, as a quarter teaspoon perhaps to a quart of distilled water. By all means add two or three pieces of charcoal to insure sweetness of the water for a long period.

As evaporation takes place, add more of the solution. After three or four weeks, start over again. Throw out the accumulation, wash vases in hot water, and set the African-violets in fresh solution. If sometimes lower leaves look gray or feel a little soft, put the plants back on plain water for a week or two. Afterwards take care to keep the water level lower. Perhaps you have exceeded the three-quarter recommendation and your plants are waterlogged. You can easily avoid this and have all kinds of artistic arrangements the water way. And in case you wish to describe this beautiful method impressively to a friend you could say, "It's done with hydroponics."

BRIEF GUIDANCE TO BLOOM (see also Chapter 3)

1. *Light.* Give all possible light and as much sun as foliage will stand without bleaching. Any window is right, if strong sunlight is filtered by a thin curtain, except in winter when full sun can be beneficial. Try "shocking" nonbloomers into flower with strong sunshine. Consider "phytoillumination," the method of growing plants under artificial light, specifically that of fluorescent lamps.

2. *Turn plants* a little each week so that all growing parts will receive about the same amount of light. Then development will be uniform.

3. *Temperature.* For daytime, try for 70 to 72 degrees F., but up to 75 degrees is acceptable; at night a drop of 5 degrees or a little less is generally considered healthful.

4. *Ventilation.* Admit fresh air once or twice daily, but *indirectly* in cold weather.

5. *Watering.* Room-temperature water or a little warmer is required. It can usually be applied from top or bottom, but *must* be from the top after a fertilizing, and often enough from the top at other times to keep fertilizer salts from collecting on the soil surface.

6. *Cleansing of foliage.* Shower with room-temperature water often enough to keep tops clean. Frequency depends on locality, once a week or once a month. Let plants dry away from sun and drafts.

7. *Humidity.* Bloom depends on enough of it. Increase the average living-room amount with pans or vases of water set on or near radiators as a source of evaporation, by grouping plants, by frequent mist-spraying, by special devices of pebble- or sand-filled saucers and trays, or with a humidifier of the cool-vapor not hot-steam type.

8. *Soil mixtures.* A mixture of equal thirds of garden loam, leafmold or peatmoss, and sand is fine; or use one of the Cornell Mixes or the all-organic Nature's Way formula. (See Chapter 3.)

9. *Soil treatment.* To prevent insect, and fungus attacks, buy treated soil. Or bake your soil mixture for one hour at 180 degrees F.

10. *Fertilizer.* Give all plants, young and old, *light,* weekly or biweekly feedings of your favorite liquefied plant food. Or just add a pinch of plant food to every watering. This method has produced almost constant bloom for me.

11. *Pot Size.* Use as small pots as plants will take without developing a matted earth ball. The "tight shoe" promotes bloom. (At least that's one opinion!)

12. *Spraying.* Pick your pest deterrent, and spray *regularly,* usually once a month. Guard healthy plants; then you won't have to nurse sick ones, or figure out ailments and what to do about them. (See Chapter 17.)

13. *"Free gifts."* Mistrust all strangers, all gift plants, all boarders. Isolate newcomers for two months before introducing them to your treasured collection. You can spot mite trouble in that time, and, if necessary, discard the one plant. Your collection will not have been contaminated.

14. *Summer quarters.* In many climates, holidays outside promote health and bloom with plants set on a porch out of wind and in shade. Plants inside must be kept as cool as possible. Air conditioning helps, especially in hot, humid climates (just don't subject African-violets to hot *or* cold drafts). In extremely hot and humid weather, keep plants on the dry side and assure good air circulation. In such weather they will probably suffer less indoors than out.

15. *Absentee care.* Ask a friend *who knows African-violets,* or at least gardening, to be your plant-sitter. Or, groom plants carefully and cover with plastic, which preserves moisture in soil and air; at the same time allow light (not direct sun) to reach plants.

2

WAYS TO ENJOY

All creatures have their joy and man has his.
George Herbert

Today the saintpaulia is the most popular of house-plants, as the rose is the best loved for gardens, and the enthusiastic societies devoted to each of these two plants have about an equal number of members.

African-violets are for everybody. Wherever you live, you can grow them; wherever you travel, you can see them. The kitchen window sill, the living-room stand, the greenhouse, the attic or basement under fluorescent fixtures, even the city apartment is hospitable to plants that are not demanding of full sun and thrive in the same pleasant warmth that we prefer.

So recently out of Africa—really less than two generations ago—the Usambara "violet" has proved to be a born internationalist. Wherever I have traveled I have seen it thriving in modest little homes as well as in commercial establishments that overflow with color. In England, France, Denmark, Norway, and Sweden, the purples, whites, and pinks, are brightly in evidence. In London I attended an African-violet club meeting and felt immediately at home. This is a friendly plant that seems to draw people into happy association.

Growers report requests for plants from distant parts of the globe—from the countries of Western Europe, Egypt, India, Japan, Australia, even the land of origin, East Africa. In this hemisphere, they ship plants successfully from Alaska to the Canal Zone, and have a lot of pleasure doing it. We agree with the nurseryman who said, "If there

18

were more African-violet fans, there would be less trouble in the world. Certainly saintpaulia-growing is a delightful occupation, and sure to bring personal contentment."

Some years ago I asked Lyndon Lyon, an eminent hybridizer, if he didn't think that African violets offered more pleasure than any other houseplant, and I have never ceased to be amused by the answer he wrote me: "Indeed I do. The African-violet offers so many possibilities. It satisfies the desire to possess, to dominate, and express maternal feelings to the fullest. It offers freedom of choice, a private little world of creation, opportunity to experiment, to prove theories, to study evolution, to meet people, to join clubs, win prizes in shows, learn parliamentary law, hold office, and start a business, large or small. It always offers something to talk about. In fact, the African-violet has something for everybody!"

TAMING OF THE AFRICAN-VIOLET

Within two years after *Saintpaulis ionantha* was discovered growing in the wilds of East Africa, it had found its way to the eastern United States via Europe. That was in 1894, but the African-violet gained no real popularity here until late in the 1930's. By the time the first African-violet society was formed in 1946, thousands of persons were eagerly seeking the knowledge that would help them grow plants soon laden with flowers. Those who possessed the ability were looked upon with awe, and for every one of them there must have been several hundred who were bewildered by the strangly temperamental African-violet.

By the early 1950's, all the mysterious "secrets" of good saintpaulia culture were becoming common knowledge, and the plant's prodigious ability to multiply became the most frequent problem. The person whose every effort to please them had once been thwarted now crowded all the windows with flowering plants. Some enthusiasts made every room in the house a haven for African-violets. At times the clutter became so great that some who might have liked to grow a few plants felt they could never set a limit, having observed friends become literally addicted to the plants. Thus, the saintpaulia became the victim of faddism.

Fortunately our noble saintpaulias have lived through that era when Homo sapiens may have at times made it almost unbearable; and now, though most gardeners consider their experience hardly complete without saintpaulias, they are content with only a few.

FIGURE 1

From *Curtis's Botanical Magazine,* 1895

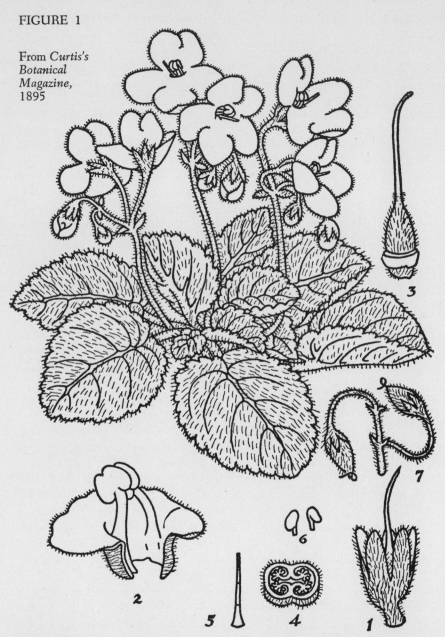

Saintpaulia ionantha. 1. *calyx and style;* 2. *tube of corolla laid open and stamen;* 3. *ovary and disk;* 4. *transverse section of ovary;* 5. *hair of margin of corolla;* 6. *ovules;* 7. *immature fruit.*

FIGURE 2

S. ionantha, Species (Modern)

While the interest in African-violets today is even greater than in the fifties, it is sane, scientific, and reasonable. Windows or basements filled beyond capacity with plants have given way to small collections of select varieties. The emphasis is on having healthy, well-groomed specimens of character and charm, and in displaying them attractively.

DECORATING WITH AFRICAN-VIOLETS

The enthusiast thinks first of providing a location that offers a hospitable climate—enough light to promote compactness and flowering, enough moisture in the soil and atmosphere to sustain leaves and blossoms, and ample warmth, with just the right amount of fresh air. Wherever these conditions can be provided in your home, African-violets can be used decoratively without any special contrivances. However, if you would like to grow plants in a place where ideal conditions do not exist, it may be possible to improve the situation by installing fluorescent lights, by humidifying a room, or in some other way discussed in this book. If you cannot grow the plants where conditions are right and then enjoy them in the same place, the solution is to provide good culture in one particular window or under lights in some convenient place, then move your best plants to enjoy temporarily elsewhere in the house.

The simplest way to decorate with African-violets is to display one specimen plant, as on a chest or coffee table. Or, group three small specimens on a lamp table by a chair or couch where you will be able to pause and appreciate them frequently. If sufficient light reaches the area to promote good growth, then watering and routine maintenance will be your only duties. If the area is poorly lighted and the atmosphere dry, it may be necessary to revitalize the plants periodically and replace them with others growing under better conditions.

When African-violets are displayed alone or in small numbers, you may want to use more decorative containers than those in which they are growing. Try slipping the pot of one plant into an attractive jardiniere that is slightly larger. This covering pot may be of any style to accord with the scheme of the room. Or group a few small plants in one larger container. I will long remember the display of African-violets I once saw in a sunny country kitchen. Five small plants covered with sky-blue flowers filled a large copper chafing dish in the center of a big table.

Or arrange a few plants on a dining table or buffet. At Christmas-time I have frequently enjoyed a tray of small African-violets in full bloom, all white singles and doubles, with evergreen sprays around the base and several candles in the center. For one dinner party I arranged single and double pinks in a rose-colored ceramic dish, 7 by 10 inches. With pale green linen and candles and green glassware, the centerpiece of plants looked charming. For another party, I clustered five lavender and purple African-violets in an ivory fan-shaped container, and the setting included white table mats, lavender candles, and amethyst glass. During hot days of summer, a grouping of African-violets, all with clear blue flowers and bright green leaves looks cool and refreshing on the dining table.

When displaying one African-violet, or several, I find that candles, or a piece of colorful fabric beneath, or a painting of just the right colors for background enhances the effect of the flowers.

Flowers and Books. A white wrought-iron stand, with trays to hold moist gravel, and double-strength glass shelves, makes a pleasant one-window setting. The stand is rolled to another window on the rare occasions when the radiator is turned on, and in summer it goes to the screened and shaded porch. *Home Garden,* Gottscho-Schleisner photo.

EN MASSE

While I enjoy one African-violet, or several together, I find special pleasure in the large collection that occupies the wide-silled windows of what was my study and is now the grandchildren's nursery. When I am busy at my desk or with housework, I often go in there for a few minutes to inspect the plants, to see the buds developing, to remove spent blossoms and leaves. Doing this I am refreshed, thankful to have nature working so close to me. I prefer to grow most of my saint-paulias by themselves, and if I introduce other plants for effect, I make sure their health is beyond question.

The pictures of my windows in this book are typical of hundreds in evidence today. I started with a few plants on the sills. Eventually this prime area became too crowded for the plants' good health, and symmetry was suffering. Then double-strength glass shelves were added above—glass so that as much light as possible could reach through to plants below. I can grow *well* about three times more plants in the windows with shelves than in those with only the sill.

In this big window garden, I never worry about how the plants are grouped, that is, how the colors are mixed, as I find most African-violets go well together. However, in other parts of the house I like to use one color alone, or similar hues massed together to enhance a color scheme. For example, in a bath where the ceramic tile is cream color, the walls papered in a gold design on white, and the towels are pink, the window is now and then bedecked with a row of pink-flowered plants, all in spotless white plastic pots.

In a contemporary house, I recall a handsome interior where saint-paulias played a vital role. Basically the room was white with furnishings of cool blue and green. An impressionistic landscape in the same colors made a dramatic effect with an elegant old teacart, painted white, and almost overflowing with azure-blue African-violets.

Teacarts and other portable stands provide excellent places for growing African-violets, and they are a boon indeed in many of today's dwellings where window sills are not wide enough to accommodate

Window Collection. This section of my window garden occupies three adjacent east windows. Behind the wooden molding, waterproof trays with white pebbles rest on the broad top of a cabinet at window-sill level. A few tall marguerites introduce a lively note of yellow, and there is a pervading fragrance from heliotrope 'Sweet Blue'. *Home Garden,* Gottscho-Schleisner photo.

flowerpots. I treasure a white wrought-iron stand of Victorian design, especially in the summertime when it is laden with violets and placed on a porch. Some growers use "violet trees." These are metal or aluminum frames in tree shape with cups or rings spaced here and there to hold pots. I find them showy in many settings, dependent of course on the quality of the plants. Pots need to be turned regularly so that all sides of every plant will be well lighted.

BUILT-IN PLANTERS

Many houses today have built-in planters in which African-violets can be used to make an area colorful. The only problem with these planters lies in lighting. If they are located where there is never any direct light, you will be wise to use foliage plants, such as philodendrons, that thrive at low intensity instead of trying to grow flowering

Complement for a Painting. Pink, lavender, and white saintpaulias in a pink ceramic container are lovely beneath Cora Brook's study of purple and white Japanese iris in a silvered frame. *Home Garden*, Gottscho-Schleisner photo.

plants. If a fluorescent fixture can be concealed 6 to 8 inches above then African-violets can be grown to perfection in your planter.

When placing them in a planter, keep them potted, and set them on a thick layer of pebbles or peatmoss. In pots, they benefit from the restricted root room which encourages profuse blooming. And if a plant becomes diseased, misshapen, or otherwise unfit for the planter, it can be lifted out without disturbing the whole arrangement.

If you want to display saintpaulias in a planter that is not well lighted, grow them in another part of the house, either in a bright window or under fluorescent lights, and let them stay in the planter only so long as they are attractive. This may be as much as a month if the atmosphere is pleasantly warm and moist.

When built-in planters are recessed in the floor in front of a window or beneath a skylight, there may be enough space for a naturalistic planting. You might use lightweight Featherock to build a terrain suggesting that in which the saintpaulia was first found in East Africa: a humid woods with some other vegetation and outcrops of limestone. You could then make lifelike groupings of African-violets at the base of a large stone or small tree, with a pebble mulch to assure clean foliage and to set off the design.

A GREENHOUSE FOR PEOPLE AND PLANTS

I will never cease to be awed by commercial greenhouses in which thousands of African-violets grow in functional, orderly rows. But I visualize something different for a hobby greenhouse. Instead of the traditional narrow paths with benches on either side, there would be plants in slightly raised beds along the sides, and the center kept open for comfortable chairs with reading lamps. Near the glass walls, some treelike plants and vines, and farther in a few large rocks for naturalistic plantings, with dozens of African-violets grouped here and there. A birdcage might hang from the ceiling at one end; supplies and tools for maintenance concealed in a cupboard.

In such a greenhouse, it would be fun to have a collection of species saintpaulias with a simulation of their natural habitat. Ideally, there would be room for some of the fascinating gesneriad relatives: perhaps the three species of *Nautilocalyx* to grow tall and luxuriant, *Gloxinia perennis* to reach its full height and produce blue, bell-shaped flowers in summer, and from a driftwood tree in one corner the epiphytic *Columnea* and *Aeschynanthus* cascading down. In the warmest wintertime spot, a collection of episcias could increase by their strawberry-like stolons and in the high humidity, bright light, and warmth they would flower most of the year.

SAINTPAULIAS WITHOUT NATURAL LIGHT

Wherever you'd like to grow thriving African-violets, fluorescent illumination makes it possible. One outstanding example of this technique, as applied to plants in decorating, is to put one or two strip fixtures 6 to 8 inches above a bookshelf in an area that is otherwise dimly lighted. Place a waterproof tray on the shelf where plants will stand, and conceal the mechanics with a 2-inch strip of painted wood; the same kind used to conceal the light fixture. African-violets and small related plants thriving in such a planter will bring lively interest to any room.

HOW TO PLANT A STRAWBERRY JAR

If you've ever seen a strawberry jar or barrel filled with semper-vivums (hen and chickens) or strawberry plants, you know what a delightful planting this can be. Happily, it works beautifully for Afri-can-violets. For this purpose, I prefer a glazed ceramic jar.

It is easy to plant such a jar. First place a stack of small empty pots in the center of the jar, half of them turned upside down, the other half resting rightside up on the first ones, and reaching to within an inch of the top of the jar. These pots assure proper drainage and aeration as well.

Remove plants from their pots and place each in its pocket in the jar. Then slowly fill up the jar with moist potting soil. Pour in a little, then tamp lightly with a ruler or a long spatula, adding more until all the plants are in place and the jar is filled. Then set one plant in the center of the top, and the picture will be complete.

After a few weeks a new planting will look attractive and natural. A well-balanced appearance is achieved only if the jar is turned every few days so that all plants receive equal light. Growing African-violets in a strawberry jar saves space and creates an ideal display. Most varieties do well this way, an exception being the big Supreme types, although one of these is excellent at the top.

Proper maintenance of a strawberry jar is important for long life. Keep the soil nicely moist (watering may be necessary only about once a week owing to the sizable volume of soil), feed the plants regularly, and trim off any spent blossoms and less-than-perfect leaves. Be particular about removing suckers as soon as they are large enough

Ceramic strawberry jar 12 inches tall provides space for 9 young African-violets. Courtesy Mrs. Horace E. Dillar, Nicholson photo.

for you to distinguish them from tiny flower buds. Keep foliage thinned away from the outside rims of plants so that part of the strawberry jar is always visible.

TOTEM POLES

Saintpaulia enthusiasts constantly seek new ways to cultivate plants both for display and to save space. One innovation used frequently in the trade for climbing philodendrons and other tropical foliage plants, is the totem pole (Figure 3). Some of these are of pressed osmunda or sphagnum moss; others are merely rough-barked pieces of tree trunk. For African-violets a slightly different totem is required.

To make the pole, get small-meshed galvanized poultry netting, 15 to 36 inches wide (depending on the height you wish the pole to be). Make a cylinder of this 6 to 12 inches in diameter. Twist the cut ends of the wire around each other all the way up the side to make a tight seam.

Then stand the mesh form upright in a pot or jardiniere. The taller the pole, the deeper this container needs to be as it serves to anchor the planting. Place the wire cylinder on the bottom of the pot or bowl. Then pour in at least 3 inches of plaster of Paris. When this hardens, in about twenty-four hours, planting may proceed.

Fill the anchored container with pebbles. These will give additional weight and serve as a catch-basin for excess moisture. Start by lining the inside surface of the cylinder above the pebbles with moist sheet moss or unmilled sphagnum. Place the first ring of plants about 4 inches up from the bottom, and at least 4 inches apart.

Take each plant from its pot, and carefully remove most of the soil.

FIGURE 3

DISPLAY AND SHOW IDEAS

If show plant dries out and leaves droop, place cardboard frame around pot edge until watering strengthens the petioles.

Make hanging basket of plastic pot by drilling three holes equidistant around the rim.

Small labels train leaves for perfect symmetry. Lower leaves in sketch need better spacing.

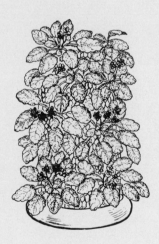

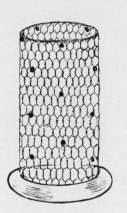

Violets grow beautifully on totem made of poultry netting lined with unmilled sphagnum moss. Add 4 inches of soil, then place first ring of plants. Continue upward, staggering plants 4 inches apart. Rotate totem often to give plants equal light.

Left, bell jars and other crystal containers make delightful planters for miniature violets.

Right, recondition old plant with long stem by rooting in vase of water.

K.BOURKE

Push roots and stem, as far up as the leaf rosette, through a hole in the wire, then through the moss. Work in enough potting soil to cover the roots, then add more moss lining.

Four inches above, place another ring of plants and stagger their positions above the first ring. When they are in place, cover the roots with soil. Continue in this way until all of the pole is planted. For most totems, it is not necessary to set a plant at the top because the upper ring of plants covers the opening there. For poles 10 to 12 inches in diameter, a plant at top center will help to give quick coverage.

African-violet totems, like strawberry-jar plantings, require several weeks of good growing before they look finished. And they too need to be rotated so that all plants receive equal light (especially important if they are standing in a window, where light comes from just one direction). Water often enough to keep the soil just moist. One way to accomplish this almost automatically is to sink a 2¼-inch clay pot, with the drainage hole corked, in the top of the totem. Keep the pot filled with water, and moisture will seep slowly through the porous clay. This source may not provide enough dampness for a tall or very wide totem, but it is adequate for a small totem and insures the plants against severe drying out in a large one.

Trim off old leaves and spent flower stalks while encouraging plants to increase in diameter until they completely cover the totem—this is different from the method for strawberry-jar plantings where we strive to keep plants so controlled that the sides of the jar can be seen. The completed totem will be covered by leaf whorls in a vertical position, with flowers hanging in bounteous clusters. If fertilized regularly, totem plantings last at least two years without the need to replant.

A BASKET OF AFRICAN-VIOLETS

If you have a sunny window or a greenhouse, flowering plants in hanging baskets make a delightful show. Most varieties may be used, but preferably those with an open habit, not kinds which incline to be compact in the way of miniatures and semi-miniatures. Use a 9- or 12-inch wire basket and line it with moist sheet moss or unmilled sphagnum. Over this spread a 2- to 3-inch layer of potting soil. Then place four plants equidistant around the basket, carefully working the roots through wire and lining until the lowest leaves rest firmly against the sides.

Add soil to within an inch or two of the top, and position four more

Well-grown African-violets in a hanging basket make a striking display. Courtesy Robert G. Anderson, Daniels Studio photo.

plants, equidistant, and alternate to those in the lower ring. Add more soil until the basket is nearly full. Then at the center, insert a 2¼-inch clay pot, the drainage hole tightly corked, and sink the pot nearly to the rim. Fill the pot with water, and keep it supplied all the time. Moisture seeping out continuously will keep the basket healthfully damp, yet it will not drip as would happen if water were poured over the top. If there is space at the top, put two small plants alongside the clay pot to conceal it and as a finish.

It takes weeks, sometimes months, before there is complete coverage of wire and moss. As with the other special groupings, plants should receive equal light. Keep old flowers and leaves trimmed away, and fertilize regularly. Apply fertilizer directly to the soil, not in the small pot used as a water reservoir.

IN GLASS CONTAINERS

Bubble bowls, brandy snifters, and stacked candy jars are some of the glass containers that offer attractive settings for miniature or semi-miniature African-violets (Figure 3). As a rule, this kind of container should be at least 8 inches across but 10 to 12 inches is better.

African-violet with round leaves grown in crystal bubble bowl on a sidetable where light is bright, but no sun strikes. Courtesy Mrs. Horace E. Dillard, Nicholson photo.

To plant, place four or five chunks of charcoal in the bottom to keep the soil sweet. Then arrange a layer of moist sphagnum moss.

Decide where you want the plant to go, and set an empty flowerpot at that place in the container. Work soil around it (a porous, open mixture) to the desired level. Firm this with your hand, then carefully remove the pot. It will leave a space into which you can slip the rootball of the plant. Finally firm the soil around the roots, adding more soil if necessary but do this carefully so as to keep leaves and petioles clean.

Give moisture sparingly to plantings in glass containers. A can with a long, slender spout makes watering easier. Tip the container in one hand, just enough so that the spout of the can nearly touches the soil when the water comes out. This procedure keeps particles of soil from spattering glass or plant.

Polish glass containers frequently with a soft cloth to keep them clean, and groom plants inside to perfection. Provide good light, but be careful that no direct sun strikes the glass or burning will result. Obviously, this is one planting that will not thrive under fluorescent lights. It is extremely pretty to bring to the living room for a special occasion or place in your guest room when a friend visits.

BOTTLE GARDENS

Bottle gardens offer another means of growing African-violets inside a glass enclosure. One planting featured a pink African-violet in a ten-gallon jug, of the type used for distilled water. A layer of charcoal chips was first placed in the jug, then sphagnum moss, and above this 3 inches of moist sterilized African-violet soil. Finally a few seeds were dropped in—from a cross-pollination calculated to give a high percentage of pinks. When the bottle was placed in the warmth of the living room on a table where the light was bright all day, but there was no direct sun, the seeds germinated quickly.

As soon as the seedlings began to grow, all but the three strongest were pulled out with long-handled wire tongs, and these three were allowed to develop until each had blossomed. Then the best one was selected and the other two carefully removed with the tongs. Thus, the best seedling grew to maturity inside the jug, like a ship model inside a bottle. When the plant was three-years-old, it produced some forty blossoms. It received bright light all the time, was watered occasionally and ever so sparingly with a little liquid fertilizer at the same time. Spent flowers and yellowing leaves were removed regularly with the tongs.

If you want to amaze your friends, and have a delightful experience, try growing an African-violet inside a bottle!

LITTLE LANDSCAPES WITH AFRICAN-VIOLETS

Small-growing saintpaulias are ideal for miniature landscapes indoors. I have in mind 2- or 3-inch-deep wooden planter boxes, or sizable plastic or porcelain trays, in which a number of plants can grow, grouped to suggest a woodland scene or a little Oriental garden with stones and gravel. Such a planting is not difficult to arrange, and may actually provide a better place for African-violets than where each grows in a separate pot of soil tending to dry out rapidly.

To make a miniature landscape, you will need a container at least 2 inches deep and 15 inches or more in diameter, and waterproof. Prepare for planting by spreading a layer of chipped charcoal, then one of unmilled sphagnum moss. Fill to within an inch of the top with African-violet soil. Then you are ready to plant. Whether or not you add plants other than miniature or semi-miniature African-violets is up to you. I enjoy a landscape that imitates a woodland scene with some other small-growing houseplants that will thrive along with the saintpaulias. Good companions for small landscapes include *Polystichum tsus-simense* (a dwarf fern), *Sinningia pusilla* (miniature gloxinia), *Helxine soleirolii* (baby's-tears), *Ficus pumila* (creeping fig), and of course miniature begonias.

I prefer these landscapes kept free of ceramic objects—Japanese fishermen, little ducks, bridges, and the like—unless the gardens are for children. Real pools can be a part of these tiny scenes. I saw one landscape kept moist by water seeping through a pool made of a corked flower pot. Baby's-tears concealed the edges, and small water-polished stones grouped here and there gave a natural appearance.

FOR THE FLOWER ARRANGER

African-violets are charming for arrangements provided their possibilities are respected. They are *small* blossoms suited to use in groupings tucked in at the base of branches or driftwood to suggest a natural planting of wild flowers at the foot of a tree. They are pleasing in small compositions for a desk, coffee table or dressing table. For miniature arrangements in the technical sense, they are ideal. The National Council of State Garden Clubs, Inc., defines a miniature as an arrangement that is "3 inches overall" including flowers, container, and base if one is used. If larger than this, they lose their peculiar jewel-like quality.

When you design a miniature arrangement, keep in mind the importance of scale. It is essential with these lilliputian compositions in which "tiny flowers and leaves and frail grasses or other foliage must be used, rather than broken-down portions of large flower clusters." Thus the individual African-violet, single or double, offers proper possibilities.

DRIED FLOWERS IN PICTURES

If you pick blossoms in perfect condition, you can dry them in a way to retain the natural color, and use later to create delightful compositions. You will need a quantity of pure white builder's sand (not sea sand), or a special flower-drying agent, such as silica gel. Spread a layer of either material 1 to 1½ inches deep over the bottom of a cardboard box. Place the flowers on this so that they do not touch, and carefully pour an inch of silica gel or sand over them. Include some buds and stems in various stages of development so that you will be able to make realistic groupings. Place the box in a cool dry place; after about two weeks, the blossoms will be ready for picture-making.

Blues and purples retain color best. Whites may turn ivory or ecru. Pinks and reds are simply less vivid than they were on the plant. Saintpaulia foliage is not suitable for drying, but the flowers combine well with dried fern fronds, the leaves of lamb's-ear (*Stachys lanata*), and small foliage from scented geraniums.

Upper left, dark and medium-blue African-violets with sprays of pink begonia buds and crocus foliage. Upper right, white, blue, and magenta African-violets with their own foliage in opaque pink bottle. Lower left, pink and white African-violets with white muscari spikes and anemone foliage in a white ceramic basket. Lower right, purple and blue African-violets in amethyst glass. Arrangements by Mrs. Fred J. Hay, Carolina Studios photo.

Miniature African-violets
on a coffee table with a
string of pearls to suggest
scale. Nicholson photo.

Before working on a picture design, choose a frame. Old-fashioned
types, particularly ovals, lend themselves nicely to dried-flower compositions. With size, shape, and style of the frame in mind, you can plan
your flower picture. Make a shadow box of cardboard, ½ to 1 inch
deep, and cover the inside with velvet, linen, paper, or whatever will
make an appropriate background for the effect you have in mind.

Handle the flowers gingerly, as they are very delicate when dried. If
your design pleases you, secure each blossom in place with a drop of
fingernail polish or household cement placed on the back. Hold gently
in place for a few seconds until the flower is firmly set. When the
picture is complete, put on a glass cover to protect the flowers. Prepared in this way, and framed, these pictures last indefinitely. They
make delightful gifts for friends who grow violets, or for anyone who
appreciates flowers—and that's just about everybody.

IN A CORSAGE

African-violets also look lovely in corsages and hold up nicely if
properly handled. Pick the flowers the day they open and "harden"
them by standing the stems in water for several hours. Arrange them
with foliage other than their own brittle leaves, asparagus or rabbit's-
foot fern perhaps. Almost any type of fern you grow will be suitable.
Insert your corsage in a lapel vase of water, and it will last well.

3

THE BASICS—SOILS, FERTILIZERS, AND POTS

More than most houseplants, African-violets are dependent on a proper soil mixture that has been treated to give protection from nematodes, mites, soil mealy bugs, fungi, and weeds. If protection is not provided at the outset, your satisfaction with African-violets is most unlikely. If it is provided, your plants will flourish with little need for spraying, certainly not more than once a month, and this would usually be simply for continuing protection rather than clean-up.

The easiest way to a reliable and fertile soil mixture is to buy it from a grower who has perfected one for his own valuable commercial crop by "sterilizing" with steam or a fumigant and adding balanced nutrients. Such soil can be purchased in packages as small as five pounds, as large as twenty-five, with a quantity price for a number of bags purchased at one time. Buying soil is really not extravagant and a very great convenience. You'd be surprised how many "experts" do this.

A GOOD SOIL

The purpose of soil is twofold—to support roots, and to supply adequate food. Soil should be of such a consistency that roots can easily penetrate, and open enough to be well aerated, that is, not so heavy or sticky when wet as to be impervious to air. Some enthusiasts grow plants in vermiculite alone, but only to support roots and provide aeration. For food, they give frequent applications of liquefied ferti-

38

lizer. Some of us use small pots, some large ones. The users of small containers consider soil mostly for support. They feed their plants about twice as much as do those whose plants grow in larger pots, which already contain an adequate amount of well-balanced, fertile soil.

Almost all African-violets will do well on the old equal-thirds formula of garden loam, leafmold or peatmoss, and sand. This mixture is light enough to be easily penetrated by the fine root system, open enough to receive air, spongy enough because of the leafmold or peatmoss to retain moisture long enough but not too long; the garden loam offers varying degrees of nourishment. If it is good enough for potatoes, it's probably balanced enough for saintpaulias.

Where your soil is very clayey, as in areas of coastal Texas, you will need to add plenty of sharp sand, or sterile Sponge-Rok, and humus to obtain a sufficiently porous mixture. Where soil is extremely sandy, as in coastal New Jersey, you might make half your mixture of humus, as peatmoss or leafmold. What you're after is a soil containing plenty of organic matter to insure easy root penetration but with water- and air-holding capacity; a pH between 6.5 and 6.9; adequate nutrition; and protection from nematodes and harmful bacteria and insects.

Many enthusiasts develop a favorite mixture and consider no amount of trouble too great in obtaining the ingredients, sterilizing as needed, and mixing.

SOIL MIXTURES

THE ORGANIC WAY

Some years ago Marie Dannemiller, a dedicated organic gardener, developed a formula she called Nature's Way. It combined peatmoss, phosphate, and potash rock, limestone, cow manure, charcoal, sand, Elkorganic, Vitaloam, and a bacterial agent like Activo to hasten decomposition. She did not sterilize any of the elements, considering that the perfect balance of her formula made it unnecessary, and she added no chemical fertilizer. Her soil mixture is still used by organic gardeners who feel we must learn to do without chemicals in this polluted world.

More conventional gardeners, but also preferring natural materials, have altered Mrs. Dannemiller's amounts a little and have also felt it necessary to sterilize some of them. Most popular, because it works so well, is Lucile Rainsberger's Nature's Way formula.* If you don't mind going to a fair amount of trouble (and most African-violet collectors don't seem to), and also special-ordering some of the materials (see Information on Supplies at the end of this book), you are pretty likely to be pleased with the way your plants respond to

Nature's Way Formula

15 pints peatmoss
 5 pints builder's sand
 2 pints dehydrated cow manure
 2 tablespoons Activo
 1 tablespoon fish meal
 2 tablespoons cottonseed meal

1 pint fine charcoal
1 pint greensand or Hybro-Tite
1 pint Ruhm's phosphate rock,
   or colloidal phosphate
1 pint dolomite limestone

The ingredients are given in order of use and the first three are sterilized, (as explained below). Now about these ingredients:

Peatmoss. Preferred is the coarse and lumpy imported German peat, a sphagnum moss, not the black sedge Michigan peat or the too fine Canadian. You could substitute this, if you have to, but counteract its fine texture with some Sponge-Rok or very coarse sand.

Sand. Builder's sand (never seashore sand) comes in several grades. You want the *coarse* type to insure drainage.

Dehydrated Cow Manure. You want a brand with granulated not a powdery texture.

Activo. Or other bacterial activator available to you.

Fish Meal (Not fish emulsion.) The meal not only adds nitrogen but speeds the growth of bacteria.

Cottonseed Meal. Used for the same purpose.

Charcoal. No. 10 is finely ground but not pulverized. It keeps the soil sweet and conserves organic nitrogen until plants can use it.

Greensand or Hybro-Tite. These forms of potash give plants the ability to utilize the nitrogen and phosphorus they require.

Ruhm's Phospate Rock. In addition to phosphorus, this form of phosphate rock contains calcium and various valuable trace elements.

Dolomite Limestone. Not by any means the same as quick-acting hydrated lime, which burns plant roots, this dolomite limestone helps to keep the soil pH (the acidity measure) at 6.5 to 7.00, the range preferred by saintpaulias.

To combine all this properly, first let the first three sterilized mate-

---

* *Gesneriad Saintpaulia News,* January–February, 1966, pp. 37 ff.

rials cool a little, then add the Activo, fish and cottonseed meals, charcoal, and greensand. Stir the wet mixture with a spoon, break up the lumps, punch holes in the mass, and let stand until really dry enough to mix by hand. (If a white mold forms, just stir it in.)

Add the phosphate rock and limestone to the barely moist mixture and mix well by hand. Let stand for a day or two longer, mix again, and store in plastic bags, or turn into a container with a cover. It is ready for potting in two weeks. This lasts indefinitely, Mrs. Rainsberger says, and properly stored isn't likely to dry out. If it does, add a little water.

She uses this mixture for "starters" ready to go into 3-inch pots and for potting larger plants, but for tiny divisions from cuttings she prefers a lighter soil.

SOIL PURIFICATION

With treated soil from a reputable grower, it is hardly necessary for home growers who have a limited number of plants to add a miticide and fungicide, provided their African-violets are not exposed to newcomer plants until after they have had a segregation period of up to two months while their freedom from pests and disease can be tested. Many of us have followed this procedure, and our small collections have kept their health.

For the fastidious and fervent who want to sterilize their own soil mixture, the usual method is by baking. Some growers, *after baking* the soil, add Dr. "V" African Violet Soil Insecticide, or V-C 13 with chlordane, four ounces to each bushel of dry soil mixture. The purpose is to get rid of undesirable soil insects, harmful fungi, and weed seeds.

To sterilize by baking, fill almost full a large roasting pan that has a cover, with your mixture of loam, peatmoss, manure, and sand. Pour enough hot water over the mixture to moisten the whole mass. Put the cover on the pan, set the oven regulator at 180 degrees, and check with your meat thermometer. Do not count the time until the correct temperature has been reached. Then bake for one hour. Don't turn the heat higher or bake any longer or you will overdo it, rendering the soil inert through excessive loss of nitrogen that occurs under very high heat; 180 degrees insures a complete killing of harmful organisms, and this is your main purpose. (Actually the degree of heat recommended "pasteurizes" rather than "sterilizes"; sterilization would destroy beneficial bacteria as well as the harmful elements. Since we are used to saying sterilizing when we mean pasteurizing, I will continue to do so throughout this discussion.)

At low temperature this baking is not likely to be such a smelly business. Mrs. Rainsberger says it is less so if the peatmoss, first put into warm water and then squeezed not quite dry, is placed in a layer at the bottom of the pan with another layer on top of the soil and manure. She sterilizes the sand separately. If you are sterilizing soil alone, better be enduring but ventilate all you can.

After the baking, let the sterilized mixture stand uncovered in a cool place for about two weeks. Stir it occasionally to insure thorough aeration. Then use it or store it for future use in a covered can. Tightly covered, it won't dry out and be difficult to handle.

FORMULAS FROM CORNELL

Two fine growing mixtures for all gesneriads (and for other houseplants, too) have been perfected at Cornell University. These formulas were prepared by Russell C. Mott who is now associated with the Bailey Hortorium of the University. He formulated these successful mixes previously when he was with the Department of Floriculture.

Use a 6-inch clay pot for measuring. There are about eighteen pots of mixture to a bushel if the soil is moderately packed, but half a bushel is a convenient amount. Anyway, don't attempt to work out amounts for less.

No. 1 Cornell Gesneriad Mix
For one-half bushel

4½ pots shredded imported sphagnum peatmoss
2¼ pots horticultural vermiculite (No. 2 or 3)
2¼ pots perlite, medium grade
2½ tablespoons limestone, dolomitic preferred
1¼ tablespoons 20% powdered superphosphate
3¾ tablespoons 5-10-5 or 6-12-6 fertilizer
1 quart Peters Soluble Trace Elements from a 1-gallon solution
    containing ¼ teaspoonful

No. 2 Cornell Epiphytic Mix
For one-half bushel

This is for the "basket gesneriads," as *Aeschynanthus, Columnea,* and *Episcia*. The finely ground firbark is manufactured by the Weyer-hauser Company. (Consult your telephone directory for the office nearest you.)

3 pots Douglas firbark, fine grind, ⅛ to ¼ inch

3 pots imported sphagnum peatmoss, shredded or screened,
⅛-inch mesh

3 pots perlite, medium grade, not coarse

4½ tablespoons limestone, dolomitic preferred

3¼ tablespoons 20% powdered superphosphate

3¼ tablespoons 5-10-5 or 6-12-6 fertilizer

1 cup Peters Soluble Trace Elements from a 1-gallon solution
containing ¼ teaspoonful

FERTILIZERS

In deciding on a fertilizing program, it is helpful to be familiar with the terms commonly used.

Organic fertilizers are those composed of once-living matter, as fish emulsion, animal manure, blood, bonemeal, hoof and horn meal; or vegetable residues—grass, leaves, stems, hay, cottonseed meal; or natural mineral products as ground limestone and phosphate rock. These are all *slow* acting.

Inorganic fertilizers are chemical products, artificially manufactured —nitrate of soda, ammonium sulfate, and muriate of potash. These are quick acting to be used with great care if you are to avoid burning your plants.

Commercial fertilizers are packaged or bagged products usually containing both organic and inorganic materials. If they are good, the proportion of organic matter is fairly large. Often this quantity is indicated, as "40 percent of the nitrogen from organic sources." All carry labeled percentages of the most vital elements. For instance a 15-30-15 means 15 percent of nitrogen, 30 percent of phosphorus, and 15 percent of potash. The remaining 40 percent is some inert carrier with little or no fertility value.

Nitrogen promotes leaf and stem strength and stimulates growth generally. Too much makes plants spindly and poor at flower production; inclined to bud drop. An excess of nitrogen may prevent varieties which normally have variegated foliage from showing their attractive coloration.

Phosphorus is for roots. It also gives a steady push to flower and seed production. Too little results in poor foliage color. Too much makes growth sappy, lacking in fiber, and weak so that the whole plant has a floppy look. Bonemeal is a good source. Allow 1 teaspoon to each 4-inch pot of soil. To promote bloom, you might water with a soluble fertilizer high in phosphorus like Peters 12-36-14.

Potassium (potash) is the antitoxin among plant foods. It wards off disease, stabilizes growth, and intensifies color. Lacking it, a plant has a dull look; flowers have no luster. Wood ashes are one source. Their strength varies with different woods. A 5-inch potful to one bushel of soil is safe.

These three basic elements, nitrogen, phosphorus, and potassium, form the basis for all "balanced" houseplant fertilizers. Although it is possible to buy packages of each element, it is usually better to purchase them already mixed in appropriate amounts.

"Trace elements"—iron, boron, manganese, and others—in small amounts are also necessary to healthy plant life. As a rule these are present in African-violet growing mediums and need not concern us here.

Do not feed ailing plants unless you have every reason to believe they are starving. Usually sick plants are suffering from almost anything except lack of food. Check the "Brief Guidance to Bloom" section at the end of Chapter 1 before you start feeding a plant that looks under par. Maybe humidity or light or watering is at fault. If for no apparent reason healthy plants fail to bloom, try this treatment: Once each week apply a solution made by mixing 1 teaspoon superphosphate in 1 gallon of water. If, after six weeks, no buds are visible, something else must be wrong, for your plants are certainly not starving.

It is a good idea to withhold food for a week or so after a big bout of blooming. Most saintpaulia plants have peaks and valleys of flowering. They require a little peace and quiet after production in order to gather their resources again. They should not be urged too quickly from their rest. This is certainly true of the larger-flowered varieties. Doubles being naturally very floriferous seem to need less rest, more food, and more water than the singles.

Weather also affects the rate of feeding. Window-sill plants require less water and less food in stretches of dull weather. Of course, plants under lights know no season and are constantly fed.

Probably the most popular—and satisfactory—fertilizers for African-violets are the various soluble types. Weekly applications are beneficial at a strength below that recommended by the manufacturer for *general* use. Usually ¼ teaspoon to 1 quart of warm water is about right for big and little plants and seedlings. It's a good idea not to depend on one brand alone, since each formula has a somewhat different chemical emphasis. Alternate two or three for best results, as Peters (very popular now), Liqua-Vita, and Hyponex, and occasionally feed with an organic material like a fish emulsion or Blue Whale, which Ernest Fisher in Canada has found so highly satisfactory. He recommends, for mature plants, in 3-inch pots, a solution of ⅓ Sturdy and ⅔ Liquid Blue Whale, applied at the rate of ½ teaspoon to 1 gallon of tepid water every seven to ten days. I prefer to give fertilizer at every watering, adding just a pinch each time to the watering can, and also alternating brands.

POTS AND POTTING

TYPES OF POTS

African-violets are so pretty and decorative in themselves that decorated containers are not really necessary, but if you have them, you will enjoy showing off a flowering specimen or two in them. However, plants look nice and thrive in plain china or glazed pots, in clay or plastic, either standard types or the azalea or bulb pans, as "squatty pots" are properly termed. Culture varies according to which kind of pot you use.

Nonporous china or glazed pots are particularly good in hot dry climates: evaporation from them is slower, occurring only at the exposed top soil, not through the sides as with clay pots. Because there is so little surface for aeration, it is wise to keep the top quarter-inch of soil in a loose condition. Work it occasionally with a fork, but don't go deep or you will damage roots. If pots have no drainage holes, provide a drainage layer of small stones or crocking (broken clay pots) with charcoal bits in the bottom, where excess water can lodge below instead of above in the soil surrounding the roots. And take care not to overwater, for soggy soil invites root rot. A porous soil mixture containing some perlite or vermiculite and broken charcoal inclines to drain quickly and is best for plants in nonporous pots. With only top watering, fertilizer salts are likely to collect on pot rims. Get rid of these as best you can with a sharp knife or a pad of steel wool.

Clay pots have the advantage of providing good aeration of soil because there is evaporation from the walls. Enthusiasts who incline to overwater plants—I know I do—might consider using clay pots because plants in them require more frequent watering than those in china or plastic.

To protect leaf stems that may rot if they rest on moist clay pot rims, coat rims with paraffin or cover them with aluminum foil.

Plastic pots are generally preferred, I think, and many of us like the squatty kinds since the root system of the African-violet is shallow, and a layer of unused soil soon sours. The plastics usually have several drainage holes so small that a *properly blended soil does not sift through* and no crocking is therefore necessary for small sizes. Furthermore, plastic pots are lightweight for handling and shipping and easy to clean.

SIZES OF POTS

Pots are graded by the measurement across the top or rim.

As for the size of the pot, it depends on the extent of the root system but many growers (not all) feel that the "tight shoe" promotes bloom. Handsome leafy specimens may develop in oversized azalea pots but no matter how attractive the plants are, how interesting their pattern and texture, they will satisfy few people as do flowers—and a lot of flowers.

Just how cramped you can keep your plants to achieve bloom depends on the space you have for them and the fertilizing program you prefer. So long as the outside of the ball of earth shows a covering of fine white roots (no brown ones, please) you should get flowers, if general culture is good. But *the earth ball should not look like a ball of white string*. When it is heavily covered with roots, it's time for shift. If you are a staunch devotee of the small-pot-and-heavy-feeding program, the pot of a large plant can be slipped into a small jardiniere or other decorative container to support its wide spread of leaves. It rather depends on how plants look best to you. Personally a great spreading specimen in a tiny pot always reminds me of a fat lady in tight shoes. The whole setup makes me nervous. I like a balanced look, and I prefer bulb pans (the squatty pots) to standard pots. I admire the plant form of the saintpaulia and feel it develops to beautiful advantage only when it has room to spread.

In any case don't overpot. Don't be *at* it all the time. Put your half-inch seedlings and your rooted leaves into 2¼-inch pots right off, and let the youngsters stay there six months to a year. Then shift to 3-inch pots or 4-inch bulb pans, and again let your plants alone. Such

Standard and Miniature African-Violets, both star types, showing comparative sizes. *African Violet Magazine* photo.

Double Peach-pink African-Violet with heart-shaped leaves, from Tinari Greenhouses. *African Violet Magazine* photo.

Centerpiece for a Dinner Party by Lucile Kile. *African Violet Magazine* photo.

Bright Pink Single Saintpaulia with Frilled Edges, developed by Fischer Greenhouses. *African Violet Magazine* photo.

quarters will be adequate for a long time, if the soil you are using is well balanced and you give extra plant food as well as fertilizer. (Of course, sick plants need to be depotted and examined. If something upsets drainage, you have to repot to set things straight again.)

The preceding paragraph is general advice that *you* must interpret. Some of the hefty Supremes only come into full beauty in 5's or 6's, but let them reach that great estate gradually, on a yearly basis, as growth indicates need. Too often people think that repotting is a panacea. They look at an ailing plant and decide right off it needs a bigger pot, or for that matter they look at a healthy one and just feel like doing something to it, so they repot.

If a plant is ailing, it probably needs *less* room. Roots may be rotted and the whole system need cutting back and repotting in a smaller, not a larger, pot. Plants usually indicate quite plainly when there is need for more room. The general appearance is not good. If it is too tall with a trunk or neck, if it is wobbly and tips over easily, if bloom production is slowing down, the plant probably needs larger quarters.

The surest way to determine this is to examine the roots. If the container has a drainage hole, gently push the plant out of the pot with a pencil. This way you won't disturb roots or break the ball of soil. If you can't get the plant out this way, it probably is severely cramped and you may have to break the pot and lift off the pieces.

SINGLE OR MULTIPLE CROWNS

Your attitude toward size of container must also be influenced by *your* preference for single- or multiple-crowned plants. Please don't let anyone tell you which you should prefer. If you like them bunchy, have them so. There are those who say that "every time you have to divide a plant because it has developed a multiple crown, you admit poor care of the plant—to let the multiple crown develop," but I don't agree. It's a matter of taste. A large multiple-crowned plant, shifted on to a 5- or 6-inch bulb pan so that it has adequate root room, can be very handsome and decorative. And cultivars developed from certain species are almost impossible to keep to simple crowns.

Show schedules generally require that exhibition plants be single-crowned, and they give real point value to a whorl of evenly spaced leaves. If you are exhibiting or prefer "single crowners," keep a watch out for suckers. Snip or rub them off with standard tweezers or a sharp pencil while they are tiny and their removal will not leave a scar. Long "splinter" tweezers are good for removing sucker growth, or the much longer type only available from a medical-supply house. Be sure, though, you aren't nudging away buds. They sometimes appear first with leaves on each side of what is to be the flower stem. If you aren't sure, wait and see development before taking action.

Considerable suckering may be a symptom of trouble or, as I have suggested, of certain species' ancestry. Crowded roots or lack of light may lead to thick bunchy growth. There may also be heavy suckering with mite infestation, a sort of desperate effort for survival. Any neglect of vital needs is likely to result in suckering, though suckering is not necessarily caused by neglect.

When you get plants from an African-violet specialist, they will usually be in 2, 2¼, or 3-inch pots. Since growers try to have budding plants for their customers, many, not all, of the saintpaulias you buy will be ready to shift on to 3's or 4's, so it's a good idea to have some larger pots or pans ready. Also have some sterilized soil at hand.

If you receive gift plants that have been supplied by a commercial florist, these will usually be multiple-crowned and in 3's or 4's. Examination may reveal a potbound condition. If so, and only if so, shift your plant on, as it is, to a size larger pot or pan, or you can separate the multiple crown into sections. Pull, don't cut apart, and when a growing unit clings stubbornly and separation will involve cutting, better leave the group as one. Too often cut plants are lost plants. If in pulling, you tear, brush over damaged areas with Fermate or dusting sulfur. Either will promote healthy healing and deter fungous trouble.

Several sections may be well spaced in the larger pot or pan, or the singles may be set individually in as small pots as possible, probably 2¼'s. If you break off any leaves in the potting process, remember each is a potential plant. Keep divided plants somewhat "on the dry side" and out of full sun till new growth indicates the divisions have taken hold. If you have little room for a collection and want numerous varieties, you had better put shifting and big plants out of your mind. Stick to 2¼'s or 3's, water frequently (usually every other day except in dull weather), and feed weekly.

As a rule a plant needs repotting about once a year. With new plants from a grower, wait three to four weeks; then shift just one plant to a pot of properly sterilized soil. If it appears to thrive after a few days, shift the rest of the plants and then put them all on your regular feeding schedule.

THE ART OF POTTING

Potting African-violets is not child's play, for foliage is brittle and to handle it safely requires infinite patience. I never work at this if I am nervous or hurried and I find if I elevate plants on inverted pots, I can more easily prevent soil from clinging to the leaves as I add it. Keeping leaves clean is indeed a hazard.

Use only clean pots. Soak *new* clay pots overnight, for the dry clay absorbs untold amounts of moisture from the soil. Sterilize *old* clay pots to avoid any carry-over of disease. Put them in a pail of boiling water with about half a cup of Clorox or use Axion, which is a grand cleanser. Let stand overnight. By morning, crusty soil and chemical salts will have been loosened enough to be easily removed with a stiff brush.

Scrub plastic pots clean in hot water and detergent, then rinse and allow to dry. One crumb of old soil can carry nematodes to a whole collection, so play safe when you use a pot that has held another plant. Water each plant well a few hours before moving it so the soil will be firm, neither soggy nor crumbly.

To depot a plant, slide your left hand over the top of the pot with the crown of the plant between your first and second fingers, grasping the rim of the pot lightly, as in Figure 4. With your right hand, invert the pot over your left and knock it against a table. Or with a pencil, push through the drainage hole to ease the plant out of the pot. Soil should stay all in one piece, without any breakage of roots. Even the bit of crocking (piece of flowerpot), should cling to the place it occupied above the drainage hole.

To shift on a healthy plant, select for it a pot one full size larger, that is, one more inch across the top, or usually somewhat less, as from 2¼ to 3. Fit an arching piece of flowerpot over the drainage hole of 3's or larger pots. Plants in smaller pots need only one piece of crocking; in tiny pots, none. Then put in half an inch, or proportionately more for large pots, of coarse soil with twiggy or stony bits in it, or arrange a layer of charcoal, small stones, or unmilled sphagnum moss. Such roughage facilitates drainage in 3-inch or larger pots.

To simplify the shifting, place in the center of the new pot a pot of the same size as the one in which the plant has been growing. If you are transplanting an old specimen with a somewhat denuded crown,

FIGURE 4   HOW TO REPOT A PLANT

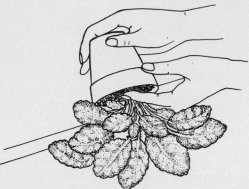

To remove plant from pot, hold soil with one hand, gently knock out against edge of table, or push out by forcing pencil through drainage hole.

When roots are cramped, transfer to larger pot or pan, adding fresh soil with spoon, then firming with stick. Leave V-shaped hole against side to receive water.

To rejuvenate a plant with decayed roots, cut away all diseased parts, pinch off all weak leaves. Dust cuts with Fermate, then set plant in a smaller pot and cover with tumbler to promote growth.

K. BOURKE

perhaps a plant that is recovering from something, set it rather low to cover up the disaster area. Fill soil in around it, and settle the soil by tapping the pot firmly against the table. This way you avoid air pockets.

Twist the center pot to firm the walls of soil around it. Then carefully remove it. A perfect mold now awaits the transferred plant. This procedure has been called the Soil Mold Method, and it has been suggested by Marie Sierk of Jacksonville, Florida. Finally fill soil in around the shifted plant being sure to leave at least half-an-inch from crown to pot rim to receive water. Leave more space for larger plants.

If removal of the pot reveals a decayed root area or your plant is suffering from crown rot, cut sharply away everything soft. Leave no speck of brown to corrupt the rest. With your fingers work away as much old soil as possible. You may not have much plant left, since you will have to remove some of the larger leaves if you reduce the root system considerably. There must be a proper balance. You can't safely prune the bottom and not prune the top. A dusting with sulfur or fermate will keep the cut areas from rotting, and a light covering with a root stimulant like Rootone will encourage growth. Repot such a reduced plant in the smallest possible pot it will take and place a drinking glass, small jar, or plastic bag over the top to give it a "greenhouse" in which to recover.

Shifted plants, as opposed to *repotted* ones, should experience no shock. They are just moving along to roomier quarters. Repotted plants were already in poor condition or they wouldn't require so much disturbance. They will come back slowly, but chances are they *will* come back.

ABOUT HOLIDAYS

IN SUMMER

In most localities, houseplants thrive on an outdoor summer. It's like camping for city children. Every element lacking or contrived in their indoor life, nature bountifully provides outside—humidity and fresh air particularly. However, if where you live, summers are so hot *you* must depend on air conditioning, let your African-violets stay inside, too. Even without air conditioning they will be better off indoors if very hot, humid weather is prolonged in your area.

Where they can go outside, *porch* summers are safer for African-violets than the open garden, no matter how shaded and protected it may be. Set plants out of strong sun and wind, and they will bloom freely and decoratively, and be thoroughly refreshed come fall. I use, among other things, my Victorian wire step-stand on the porch where African-violets look charming with the philodendrons from indoors.

Perhaps you will have some expendable saintpaulias from seed sown the previous fall or winter. Why not treat these as annuals? After the weather has warmed, select a spot outdoors that has protection from strong sun and wind. I once had a little ell between house and garage where cast-off African-violets grew through the summer in lovely association with lacy ferns and other woodsy plant life. A mulch of stone ships arranged under each leaf spread prevented mud spattering. The plants gave some bloom even in the heat of midsummer, and they were expecially lovely during the more temperate days prior to frost. Even after light frost, they gave a little bloom. I called this my installment plan for getting rid of healthy but unwanted African-violets—it seemed less ruthless than discarding from the window garden directly to the compost pile.

There are ways to make summers more pleasant for saintpaulias that stay indoors. Keep them as cool as possible. One Kansas grower moves all of her plants to the basement and grows them under fluorescent lights until the cool days of autumn. She keeps the basement windows closed during the day when outside air is hot and dry, but opens them at night. Another, who lives in Texas near the Gulf, keeps plants on the dry side, and is especially careful to provide ample air circulation throughout the summer. She has found that moist soil combined with high temperatures and too much humidity brings on fungus trouble. In addition, she keeps central air conditioning on about twelve hours out of every twenty-four during really torrid weather, and this benefits her African-violets.

Experts differ on whether or not African-violets need to be fed in summer. I maintain my regular feeding schedule, except during periods of extreme heat (day after day above 85 degrees F.); then fertilizer is withheld. Following this practice, my saintpaulias reach the cool days of autumn in much better condition than if they had been starved all summer.

If you live in hot areas in this country, you can provide a lathhouse for your African-violets. So long as night temperatures do not go much below 60 degrees F., they will be safe—and look lovely with such plants as fuchsias, ferns, and philodendrons. The lath strips must be placed close enough to ward off noonday sun, and if the summer is dry, considerable misting under the benches or stands will be necessary to increase humidity. These lathhouses, possible in such places as Hawaii, and the southern parts of California, Texas, and Florida, are the envy of every visiting gardener from the North and East. Going into the small flowery "rooms" is like entering a corner of the Garden of Eden.

ABSENTEE CARE

There comes a time when you must leave your African-violets, perhaps for a few days, a two-week vacation, or a trip to Europe. The obvious thing to do is ask a friend to be your plant-sitter. Actually, unless this person knows the ways of saintpaulias, or is at least a good gardener, you may be better off to leave your collection untended.

African-violets *can* be left alone for a few days, or up to several weeks. One way to do this is to cover them as a group with a large sheet of polyethylene (such as a painter's drop sheet) or individually with a tent of Saran Wrap or other plastic, as in Figure 5. Here are the keys to success with this method.

1. Locate plants where they receive bright light, but no direct sun. (If they are under fluorescents, set a timer to turn the lights on and off each day.)

2. Strive for temperatures on the cool side, say 60 to 68 degrees F., and if you must be away in summer, grouping plants on the basement floor may be the best you can do. When fluorescent-lighted plant carts are covered with polyethylene, the temperature inside may reach 80 degrees F. even though the room is a cool 68. However, if plants inside were healthy to begin with, and you follow steps 3, 4, and 5 below, the heat probably will do no harm.

3. Have soil just nicely moist, *not wet,* before covering with plastic.

4. Remove all old leaves that are beginning to discolor or droop, *and all flowers including buds* that are large enough to open while you will be away. Any flowers that fall on leaves under these conditions of high humidity may provide a breeding place for fungus spores.

5. Before you leave the plants under wraps, inspect each to be certain it is free of insect and disease; any plant not healthy may be treated and isolated from the rest, or destroyed; do not place it with healthy ones.

As an absentee grower, don't expect your plants to be perfectly symmetrical when you return—unless they were *directly* beneath

FIGURE 5

HAPPY VACATION!

Porous clay bricks or a 2-inch stack of newspapers, almost but not quite submerged in water, as in a tub, provide a steady source of moisture for clay pots that rest on them; good for about 2 weeks.

Plants grouped together with pots surrounded by wet sand, peat-moss or vermiculite will remain in good condition for 14 days or more. Provide light and fresh air.

One way to leave violets unattended for as much as several weeks is to cover them as a group (left), or individually (above), with plastic held up by wire or bamboo stakes. Plants will thrive on the extra humidity.

K. BOURKE

54

adequate fluorescent light. But they will be alive, thriving in the increased humidity, and even in new bloom. A vacation may be good for the plants as well as for you!

There are other ways to leave African-violets untended for several days, up to two weeks, without covering with plastic. One Pennsylvania woman follows this plan: She fills a shallow carton on the basement floor with wet sphagnum moss. The African-violets are allowed to become quite dry before the pots are packed close together in the moss. Old leaves, all blossoms, and advanced buds are removed; then the plants are watered thoroughly. With a window open to allow air circulation, the plants get along well without any attention whatsoever for fourteen days or more.

One of my neighbors is able to leave safely a small collection of various houseplants, including African-violets, by grouping them in the bathtub. The key to his method is the porosity of clay pots—other types wouldn't work. He fills the tub with about 2 inches of water, and then places several red bricks on which to set the clay pots as in Figure 5. Moisture seeps up slowly but surely through the bricks to the pots, which in turn keep the soil healthfully damp for at least two weeks.

And there is the wick way, using long wicks and adequate vessels of water (see Chapter 1).

4

LIGHT, FIXTURES, AND SETUPS

The thing to do is to supply light not heat.
Woodrow Wilson

In the early days of our excitement, we all wanted a greenhouse for our expanding collections of African-violets. Then a few enthusiasts discovered the possibilities of fluorescent light. They found that poor-flowering, even non-blooming, window-sill plants would produce almost without ceasing once they became acclimated—in about a month—to a proper number of light hours and were given good culture under fluorescent tubes. Best of all with these overhead lights, which are also called lamps, space for plants was tremendously increased. Basements in particular could be made into extensive garden rooms; an unused closet—if there was such—could be fitted up for plants; and small areas in bookcases and kitchens could become decorative little plant alcoves.

Phytoillumination is a term referring to light directed upon a plant (*phyton*). Photosynthesis means the manufacture of chemical compounds by radiant energy. The tissues of all green plants contain chlorophyll, which by photosynthesis manufactures carbohydrates, essential for the plant's growth.

At a window a plant receives just as much light as exposure, weather, and season permit. Under contrived phytoillumination the amount of light can be constant and regulated according to the needs

56

of the plants. And these needs vary greatly. In my Plant Room, for instance, saintpaulias thrive under lights that are kept on for twelve to fourteen hours; some growers report success with just ten hours; others with twelve; some keep lights on for sixteen hours. The point is, African-violets are "daylight neutral plants" and will bloom under a fairly wide range of light hours.

Not so the poinsettias in the same room but not under lights. These are short-day or long-night plants. To get them to set buds, I hustle them off to a dark closet at 5 P.M. and do not waken them until 8 A.M. the next day, and this goes on for six weeks from mid-October to December. Poinsettias bloom only with a reduced photoperiod; obviously African-violets require a longer photoperiod, but just how much light do they need, and how can we measure the amount we are supplying?

THE FOOTCANDLE

Right here we run into the mystery of the footcandle. This is the unit of measurement used by illumination engineers. It is an extremely difficult unit for the horticulturist to translate into practicalities. In laymen's terms, a footcandle is a unit of illumination equivalent to that produced by the light of one "international candle,"* evenly distributed, at a distance of one foot. The footcandle measures only the yellow/green portion of the visible spectrum, the light we humans see by. In summer, intensity of sunlight may exceed 10,000 footcandles; in midwinter 5,000; on cloudy days 1000 to 2000; in smog or haze 300 to 400. African-violets do not require the high intensity of a summer's day, as do geraniums and roses.

Natural daylight is made up of different color bands in certain proportions. In the rainbow, we see light separated into its color components. With the use of a spectrograph, we can measure the red/blue areas either in daylight or in artificial light. Footcandle meters, and they are indeed expensive, measure for us only the yellow/green components (our eye-sensitivity region). Furthermore, at this point in research it would seem that the green/yellow component that human vision depends upon is of little use to plants. Important for them are the violet/blue and orange/red properties of light. The violet/blue

---

* The "international candle" itself is a unit (not a candle), being the intensity of light emitted by 5 square millimeters of platinum at the temperature of solidification.

affects the direction of plant growth and also promotes sugar-and-starch manufacture by the chlorophyll. Orange/red light affects germination, vegetative growth, and time of flowering; also photosynthesis (the production of plant food), just as the violet/blue does.

The point of all this is that in selecting lights, we must choose among the fluorescent tubes for which claims are made on the basis of their color emphasis. And then there are the incandescent lamps to consider. It is indeed puzzling to know the right tubes and lamps to buy.

WHICH TO BUY

Artificial light for plants is, of course, supplied by the two sources commonly used for seeing—the incandescent bulb and the fluorescent bulb, tube, or lamp. The familiar incandescent bulb gets very hot; in fact, a great deal of the energy it produces is heat and not light. Such heat can burn plants that come too close and may even heat the bench if there is little circulation of air around it. And there is the hazard of exploding a hot bulb if cold water touches it. If incandescent bulbs are used, they should be the type manufactured for ovens or outdoor light fixtures.

The fluorescent tube is long and cylindrical rather than pear-shaped. This tube produces light when the phosphors with which it is coated become excited. The fluorescent tube does not get hot; it does get warm, and plants should not be placed too close or leaves will burn or be deformed.

The special tubes manufactured for plant growth are modifications of the white fluorescent lamps. They are formulated with more than the usual amount of the phosphors that produce the red/blue light, the light that plants use for growing. In the original Gro-Lux tubes the predominance of these colors produced a lavender glow. Recent developments of the Gro-Lux tubes have included enough of the yellow/green to produce a pleasant pink-white light.

The new growth tubes have had wide acceptance, although experience has shown that lovely blooming African-violets and other gesneriads can be grown without special tubes and without incandescent bulbs; we did so long before the special tubes came on the market; cool whites, natural, and daylight tubes were used extensively, and some hobbyists still prefer them. The terms apply to the kind of light a lamp produces. For instance, a "cool white" is not a tube that is cool but one that produces a light that looks cool; a "natural" tube hardly

FIGURE 6

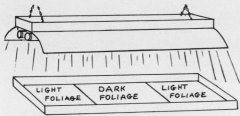

Violets with light foliage thrive toward the ends of fluorescents, those with dark leaves prefer center area.

L. to r., timer turns lights on and off, thermometer gives temperature, hygrometer tells percentage of relative humidity.

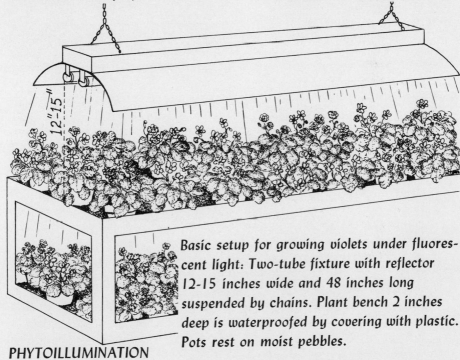

12"-15"

Basic setup for growing violets under fluorescent light: Two-tube fixture with reflector 12-15 inches wide and 48 inches long suspended by chains. Plant bench 2 inches deep is waterproofed by covering with plastic. Pots rest on moist pebbles.

PHYTOILLUMINATION

Fluorescent strip fixtures may be installed over bookcase shelves.

K. BOURKE

The Starlite Table Top Lamp is a perforated copper-toned shade through which come sparkling little points of light. The time switch at the right requires no installation, is simply plugged in. Set for the hours of light you determine, it automatically turns lights on and off. Floralite Co. photo.

duplicates the sun's rays; and a "daylight" tube does not produce daylight. Natur-Escent by Duro-Lite is a "full-spectrum tube—the closest to natural outdoor light—that eliminates all color distortion." The light is very pleasing, I think.

The advantage of the growth lamps, which cost about twice as much as the standard whites (because the phosphors used are more costly), lies in the amount of *usable* radiant energy produced for plant growth. Many consider them superior for seed germination and seedling growth because of their output in the blue and red regions of the spectrum. Sylvania claims that the usable red energy in the standard Gro-Lux lamps is about three times that of a cool white lamp, and the blue energy is about twenty-five percent greater. With their Gro-Lux lamp, the company advises for germinating seeds and root cuttings: 10 lamp watts per square foot at 6 to 8 inches above soil level for 16 hours; for newly germinated seedlings and rooted cuttings, prior to transplanting, up to 20 hours; for low-energy plants, like the saintpaulia, 15 lamp watts, 12 to 15 inches above the plant tops.

Because of the heat produced by incandescent lamps, their use has been seriously questioned for plants in the home. The recommendations of the USDA and certain universities have not been considered helpful because the air-cooling of the control boxes in which the test plants were grown would not be generally available. In this regard, the comparative tests with cool white and Standard Gro-Lux lamps with incandescents carried out by Vernon A. Helson at the Plant Research Institute at Ottawa, Ontario, Canada, are interesting.* The

---

* Vernon A. Helson, "Growth and Flowering of African Violets under Artificial Lights," *Greenhouse-Garden-Grass*, Vol. VII, No. 2 (Summer, 1968).

plants were in growth cabinets in a large room where the light temperatures were around 25°C [77°F] and the dark temperatures around 20°C [68°F], the relative humidity about 30 percent. The temperature in the cabinets was not controlled. Mr. Helson reached these conclusions:

"Fifteen watts per square foot of fluorescent light giving about 300 footcandles are adequate for good vegetative growth and flowering of African-violets.

"Gro-Lux fluorescent lamps with some incandescent light produce more vegetative growth and more flowering than cool white with incandescent or cool white or Gro-Lux alone.

"Flowering of African-violets is increased when the far-red from incandescent light is added to either Gro-Lux or cool white fluorescent light.

"Also, Gro-Lux lamps may have an aesthetic value for the hobbyists in that the high blue and red emitted by the lamps causes the leaves to appear darker green and the flowers a brighter red or blue."

Sylvania now offers the Wide Spectrum Gro-Lux lamp. This was first designed for greenhouse use and for high-energy plants like roses and geraniums, not for the low-energy saintpaulia. In addition to

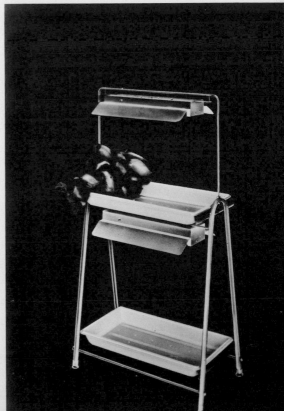

The Sunlighter Plant Stand with rustproof trays, lighted by fluorescent lamps, accommodates a number of plants in a small space. Sylvania photo.

"major energy in the blue and red, it produces far-red energy." If you use this Wide Spectrum lamp, it will not be necessary to use incandescent lamps as well. The same is true of Duro-Lite's Natur-Escent tube. This "produces the desired effect without the need for mixing with other fluorescent or incandescent tubes."

These growth tubes can be used alone or, except for the Wide Spectrum lamps, in any combination with standard tubes that suits you. A popular choice of the conventional tubes is one daylight and one natural tube, but with these two you get a quantity of useless green/yellow and less of violet/blue and orange/red than the growth tubes supply, as is shown in the table below.

Relative Qualities of Lights

Name of tube	Violet/blue needed by plants	Green/yellow not needed by plants	Orange/red needed by plants
Cool white	good	excellent	good
Daylight	excellent	very good	deficient
Warm white	deficient	good	very good
Natural	deficient	good	very good
Gro-Lux	excellent	deficient	excellent
Gro-Lux Wide Spectrum	excellent	some	excellent
Natur-Escent	excellent	good	excellent
Plant-Gro	excellent	good	excellent

FIXTURES

In planning any fluorescent setup, it is essential to allow *15 to 20 watts of illumination for each square foot of growing area.* Thus a plant table or shelf 1 × 4 feet in dimension, that is, containing 4 square feet, can be adequately lighted by two 48-inch, 40-watt tubes, set side by side in a 12- or 15-inch reflector. With this amount of light, African-violets will bloom and bloom, regardless of weather or season.

The fixtures to hold the tubes determine the size of the tubes to buy. For instance, a 20-watt tube fits into a 2-foot fixture; a 40-watt tube fits into a 4-foot fixture; and a 75-watt tube fits an 8-foot fixture. Generally speaking, it is best to use the longest tube possible to fit your space since this will be the most efficient.

Different types of fixtures also determine the type of tube to buy. Some fixtures have starters, the newer ones do not, these are called "rapid start." Rapid-start tubes work in either type of fixture; but a tube requiring pre-heating must be used in the fixture with the starter. Sylvania also puts out a Gro-Lux circleline tube that can be fitted into the familiar kitchen-ceiling fixture. Two interesting fixtures for plants have been designed with this tube. When the bowl or pan is filled with African-violets, a charming decoration results for the home or office (where it could be distracting to the thinker).

REFLECTORS AND FILMS

Reflectors help to direct the light. They can be made from cardboard or metal bent to proper angles for attaching to industrial strip fixtures which do not come with built-in reflectors. You can paint the underside of these homemade reflectors a *flat white* (not enamel) rubber-base paint to intensify the light given back to the plants.

Although the existing wiring of most dwellings can accommodate the addition of several fluorescent lights for plants, don't add more than two or three units until you have consulted your electrician or local utilities people. An overload on the wiring can at best cause a tripped breaker switch or blown fuse, and at worst a fire. The cost of burning fluorescents for plants is unbelievably low considering the satisfaction they give. For an accurate estimate, ask your local power and light company. Rates vary considerably from one area to another.

This 1969 estimate comes from the Union Electric Company of St. Louis, Missouri: The cost of operating one two-lamp fixture (two 40-watt lamps) for a 14 hour day is 2.8¢ (2 mills per hour) or 84¢ per month. One three-lamp fixture (using 40-watt lamps) would cost 4.2¢ per day or $1.26 per month. Four 40-watt fluorescent lamps used for a 14-hour day would cost approximately 5.6¢ per day or $1.68 per month.*

Sylvania estimates that "a single 4-foot Gro-Lux lamp operating for fourteen hours per day on a 2½ cents per kilowatt rate would use less than 12 cents worth of electricity per week." And the estimate for Natur-Escent is the same.

Greenhouse growers may find it practical to install fluorescent units above under-bench areas. When this is done, growing space may be

---

* *African Violet Magazine*, Vol. XXIII, No. 2 (January, 1970), p. 41.

almost doubled. However, when African-violets are placed directly on a greenhouse floor, roots may get too cold in winter for good growth. This can be avoided by installing heating cables under the sand or gravel on which pots will rest. If thermostatically controlled, the cables will operate only when needed. Many greenhouse growers now supplement natural light with fluorescent during cloudy weather or through the short days of the year. Fixtures are installed in any part of the greenhouse where more light is needed.

SELECTING FIXTURES

The complaint against fluorescent-light growing is that plants cannot be displayed decoratively. For many enthusiasts this doesn't matter at all. It's the growing they enjoy, and a big basement area filled with flowering plants is completely satisfying. In fact, more basements than living-rooms are used, for the average living-room cannot contain all the plants that a confirmed African-violet hobbyist wants to grow.

For plants-with-people various floral carts and movable stands are possibilities. Some are made like an old-fashioned tea cart; others are add-a-shelf arrangements fitted for fluorescent growing. Some also have outlets for incandescent lights. No special wiring is required; you just plug in the carts or stands to an outlet as you would a lamp or toaster. Filled with blossoming African-violets, they are a lovely sight and they are not necessarily lighted by day. If the fluorescent glow does not seem agreeable, lights can just as well be turned off by day and on by night, but only if no less than six hours of total darkness is provided in the daylight period.

For small displays, there are portable table-top units fitted with fluorescent tubes. These are nicely designed. Under them set plastic trays to hold the plants above a humidifying layer of moist gravel, perlite, or vermiculite. Be sure to select fixtures with two tubes; a single 15- or 20-watt lamp won't do much for culture if it has to illuminate more than one square foot.

Attempts have been made to produce screens and room dividers with lights and shelves for plants. Attractive as these are for decoration, they haven't really solved the problem as far as the low-growing saintpaulias are concerned because the lights are set too far above plants for good growth. Where a large single reflector with growth lights can be suspended by chains or set on legs above a broad window sill, counter, table, or chest, a very pretty and practical display can be arranged. Carts, table-top pieces, hanging lights can be purchased

Adequately lighted by a concealed 40-watt fluorescent tube, African-violets thrive in this section of a bookcase, and are a pleasant contrast to the volumes on shelves above and below. If a plastic, pebble-filled tray is used instead of saucers, more plants can be grown in the same space. Roche photo.

from saintpaulia specialists, local garden centers, and mail-order houses. (See Information at the end of this book.)

HOME CONSTRUCTIONS

A carpenter or do-it-yourselfer can also fix up many places around a house for small African-violet gardens. These are a joy to the enthusiast who likes flowers at every turn, and of course, wants plants in prime condition. A section of bookcase can be wired for plants and finished off with molding fastened at the top to conceal the tubes, and at the bottom to hide the tray of perlite, or whatever, on which plants are set. Sometimes a section of kitchen counter can be sacrificed for a fluorescent garden, or a deep drawer removed from a chest, the interior fitted with lights and trays for plants.

Important in planning these household displays is the selection of space of a size to accommodate standard equipment. Since 15 to 20 watts of light per square foot of growing space is essential, you will want 40- or 72-watt tubes. Fixtures for lesser wattage are available, but it's always a problem to find tubes to fit. The "strip" type fixture is best for cabinets where the inside can be coated with *flat* white paint to serve as reflector.

More ambitious for the home handyman is the bench designed by Alfred Katzenberger for two trays of plants with lights over each (Figure 7). The trays are of wood, the frame of the same kind of tubing as is used to hold electrical wires. Angle irons would also be suitable. This bench is 48 inches high, the trays 18 by 23 inches.

It is important not to build so high that you must climb to reach the plants, nor so low that you must kneel to care for them. Width should be no greater than the reach of your arm. So maximum and minimum sizes depend upon your own physical stretch and also upon the space in which the bench will be standing.

If possible, counterweight the light fixtures to make them move up and down easily. You can do this with pulleys and window-sash chain. The possibility of pulling lights up and out of the way while you water, spray, and work with the plants makes a bench infinitely more convenient.

LIFE OF LAMPS

One last point: standard fluorescent lamps do not last forever, but burned, as they usually are for saintpaulias, for 10- to 14-hours stretches, they do last a long time, the effective growth-factor rating being given as 5000 to 6000 hours by Sylvania. They wear out much faster if turned on and off for short periods of say three hours or so. It is during the first 100 hours of light that there is the greatest loss, some 10 percent, as you can easily notice if you compare the light from a new lamp with that from one you have used for up to 100 hours. Thereafter the decrease is less to 500 hours, about 25 percent, and then considerably more as the hours mount up to the service rating.

If you observe a general slowing up of growth and bloom, it may be

FIGURE 7

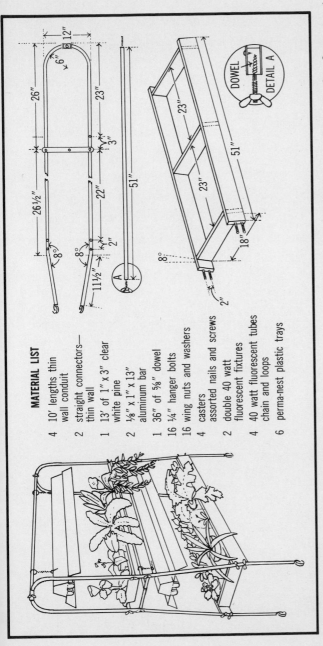

MATERIAL LIST

4 10' lengths thin
   wall conduit
2 straight connectors—
   thin wall
1 13' of 1" x 3" clear
   white pine
2 ⅛" x 1" x 13"
   aluminum bar
1 36" of ⅝" dowel
16 ¼" hanger bolts
16 wing nuts and washers
4 casters
   assorted nails and screws
2 double 40 watt
   fluorescent fixtures
4 40 watt fluorescent tubes
   chain and loops
6 perma-nest plastic trays

DESIGN FOR A FLUORESCENT CART

(Courtesy *Flower & Garden* magazine)

This bench was designed for simplicity, low-cost, and availability of materials. A tube-bender was used to shape the four legs at the tops and the 8 degree offset 11½ inches from the bottom. (A hardware store or electrician can do this for you.) For the two pieces of conduit at right angles, see detail A. A 3-inch stub of maple dowel is hammered into the end of the conduit. (The diameter of the dowel depends upon the inside measurement of the conduit.) About 2½ inches from the end, drill through the metal only a slightly larger hole than the small locking screw; drill a smaller hole for the screw in the wood. Then at the end, drill a hole into the dowel in the center. Make it slightly smaller than the thread and screw in the hanger bolt, putting the coarse thread into the wood. Tighten bolt with pliers at center serrations.

Where the hanger bolts go into the wood framing, use the same method. After assembling the top part of the structure, apply enough pressure to spring the legs apart so they will fit the wood frame. This pressure plus the holding ability of the bolt connectors makes a rigid stand. For a better appearance, you can replace wing nuts with acorn nuts.

67

that the tubes are aging, or they may simply be dirty. A coating of dust or grime is bound to reduce light. Try to make it a practice to clean tubes and fixtures about once a month. But if standard tubes have been in use for 15 to 18 months, and growth tubes for about 12 months, or if dark rings appear at the ends, replacement is definitely in order. And don't think because you see well enough by used tubes that the light is adequate for plant growth and bloom. You can read well enough with a minimum of fifty footcandles; plants need much more light.

When you put in new tubes (at first set a little higher above plants than the old tubes were), you will notice a real spurt of growth due to the increase of light. In any case, if you are trying fluorescent culture for the first time, expect to experiment a little. You know light is not the only requirement, though a very important one, for African-violets. A perfect balance of other factors is essential along with light, particularly adequate humidity, proper watering, and timely fertilizing.

5

CULTURE UNDER
LIGHTS

Truly the light is sweet, and a pleasant thing it is . . .
Ecclesiastes XI, 7

African-violets grown under fluorescent lights require
the same culture as those in natural exposures—only more of it! The
plants work harder, stimulated into producing almost constant bloom,
hence their needs are greater. No dull period checks activity as with
plants subject to the weather and the seasons.

Early experience with lights was often disappointing because the
increased needs were not recognized. Now it is well known that plants
grown this way require more water and more nutrients. Of course,
heat and humidity must be kept at the same good levels as in daylight.
Plants may be watered from above or below, according to your convic-
tions, and light misting is agreeable if the reflectors can be lifted to
permit this, or if there is adequate distance between plants and tubes
for you to manage spraying without having to move all the pots. You
may have to move them anyway about once a month if you spray to
deter insects and disease. Interestingly, if you use warm water for
misting and spraying, foliage under lights dries without spotting, as it
is likely to do if exposed while wet to strong natural light or sun.

Because of their flat type of growth, African-violets are ideally
suited to fluorescent culture, the whole spread of foliage easily reached
by the light. And how nice it is not to have to give that weekly quarter-
turn to promote balanced growth at the window!

69

An overhead Bloom Lamp fixture is adjustable from 8 to 24 inches and includes both fluorescent and incandescent lamps. House Plant Corner photo.

AMOUNT OF LIGHT

Fluorescent tubes do not emit the same amount of light throughout their length. Light comes strongest from the center, falling off at the ends. Because of this, you want to select as long a tube as possible, to have the advantage of a long bright center.

Light requirements vary with African-violet varieties. Some need more light than others. Experience is the best guide as to where to place your plants on your shelf or bench—in the center for maximum exposure, at the ends of the tubes for less. To give examples by varietal name is not feasible, but here is a rule of thumb: The darker the leaf the more light it will usually absorb, so place dark-leaved varieties under the center of the lights. Plants with pale leaves and white or light-colored flowers, also miniature plants, should *generally* go at the ends of the tubes on the outer edge of bench or shelf. But this is not a hard-and-fast rule because some varieties will surely contradict it.

To determine if your plants are getting too much light examine the foliage. Bleached or paler-than-normal leaves are one indication; another is leaves turning downward and hugging the pot in an effort to draw away from the light. Bunching, which closely resembles mite damage, in the center of some varieties, especially the "girls," is usually due to too much light. And if variegated plants turn green, the reversion may also be due to too much light.

On the other hand, inadequate light will show in the normal ways a plant indicates that its situation is too dark. Leaves will stretch upward, petioles will be overlong. Flowering will be scarce, or there will be no budding at all. Moving plants with these symptoms to brighter locations will result in a dramatic improvement, provided, of course, that the problem was only one of too little light and that other cultural requirements were met.

DISTANCE AND HOURS

There can be no hard-and-fast rules since intensity of light from the tubes varies so much, and temperature and humidity are contributing factors. The distance between plants and lights must also be taken into consideration. Measure from the *top of the plant,* not from the shelf or from the top of the pot. General experience indicates that a good distance for mature plants with dark foliage is 6 to 8 inches under white lamps, about 10 inches below the growth lamps, but distance is really dependent upon plant response. Claims are also made for a 3- to 4-inch distance (see Chapter 13 on show plants), but when I tried this, my plants were scorched. My own experience under growth lamps seems to be most favorable at 7 inches for standard plants, 5 inches for miniatures, temperature at 72 degrees F., humid-

The metal pan of this Ripe-N-Grow Sun-Lite fixture—originally designed for fruit—holds a decorative display of African-violets arranged by Anne Tinari, and the plants grow well under the 22-watt wide-spectrum fluorescent circline tube. Tinari Greenhouses photo.

Anne Tinari makes a charming decoration of African-violet plants set on a layer of pebbles in the white plastic bowl of Sylvania's Sun-Bowl Desk Lamp Planter. The wide-spectrum Gro-Lux 22-watt circline tube provides enough light for growth even in a modern office without windows. Tinari Greenhouses photo.

ity 40 to 45 percent. For seedlings 6 to 8 inches above the soil would be about right. But make haste slowly. Don't expose window-sill plants to full, close illumination in one great leap. Start with lamps well above the 6 to 8 preferred inches if lights can be so adjusted. Then over a period of seven to ten days move the lights closer and expose the plants longer. Don't fertilize during this get-acquainted period but watch watering to prevent the plants from drying out.

You might start with 10 hours of illumination and work up to the usually acceptable 12 to 14, even to 16 hours. My plants, standards and mini's, rarely get more than 14 hours. (If the plants' light-hours are too long for you and you go to bed early to read, you'll have to get up and turn off the lights, unless you have a timer!) Again, experiment with hours and distance and be guided by your plants' response.

Because 10 to 14 hours of light are productive, don't think 24 hours would be better. For good health, insure a period of darkness, at least six hours of it. A 24-hour period of light would be harmful to your plants. In very hot weather when plants are likely to stand still and not even open well-formed buds, fewer hours than you usually allow will probably be adequate, say 10, if you regularly allow 12 hours.

Miniature gesneriads, such as *Sinningia pusilla*, thrive with the same amount of light as saintpaulias, but most standard-sized gesneriads generally require more light. For instance, if you are growing episcias for flower and not just for foliage, it will be necessary to place them right in the center of the shelf where they can receive light from all sides as well as from above. Gloxinias, however, need more light than African-violets. Columneas look nice hanging over the edges of shelves but they won't bloom well that way, unless you install a vertical bank of lights facing the leaves so they can perform their important function of making food.

Experience and a little experimentation are the best guides to satisfaction with plants under lights. There are so many variables in every situation; you will need time and patience to hit upon the best schedule for *your* particular setup. Distance from lights cannot be exactly prescribed, only suggested—it could be 3 inches, it might be 10—and the same is true of light hours—10 to 16 hours are all possibilities. But two things are certain: culture under lights must be just as good as in any other situation, and the greater needs of plants as to food and water provided for under growth-lamps more food is needed than under conventional lamps.

If your plants aren't responding as they should, check over your schedule and try improving it in various ways.

AFRICAN-VIOLETS ON THE MIDNIGHT SHIFT

In parts of this country where summer heat and humidity present a problem with African-violets, some fluorescent growers burn the lights at night, leave them off in the daytime. One grower who works with

This movable 52-inch FloraCart is equipped with two standard 25-watt incandescent bulbs spaced between two 40-watt fluorescent lamps for each shelf. Tube Craft photo.

his plants only at night strives to maintain a daytime temperature range of 60 to 63 degrees F. in winter while the lights are off, and keeps the temperature at 68 to 73 degrees F. during the 14 hours of evening, night, and early morning while the lights are on. Thus he is able to enjoy his indoor garden after dinner in the evening, but while the plants' day is still young. The business person can let a timer turn the lights on several hours after he leaves the house in the morning, and return that evening to find the plants thriving under perfect light.

Some growers are careful not to switch on lights for more than a few minutes during the period of darkness. I have not found that an occasional hour or two of illumination during the plants' nighttime did damage, but experience with poinsettias indicates that darkness interrupted, even briefly, affects bud-set adversely, and the same could be true of saintpaulias during their shorter dark stretch. As I have stated before, leaving lights on continuously will be harmful.

VOICES OF EXPERIENCE

Keeping a basement warm enough for African-violets in winter is often a problem, especially for those who live in severely cold climates. One grower in Manitoba, Canada, solved the dilemma by burning the lights at night when the furnace was turned down for sleeping comfort upstairs. The heat given off by the lights, while slight, kept the temperature range agreeable for saintpaulias. This arrangement combined perfectly with the family's schedule since the furnace was turned up in the daytime while the lights were off.

A Kansas City grower met the problem similarly. He found it necessary to cover his FloraCarts with polyethylene to promote humidity and keep up warmth while the house was cooler at night. Even though nighttime basement temperatures dropped to nearly 60 degrees F., inside the polyethylene covers, plants basked in perfect light and enjoyed 72-degree temperatures and 50 percent humidity.

A woman in Seattle who had a fluorescent basement setup was concerned about damage which looked like that caused by mites. The trouble occurred when the winter temperature stayed near 60 degrees F., humidity at 40 percent, with biweekly feedings. When an examination of the ailing plants revealed no insects, she changed procedure. She cut down fertilizer to one application every six weeks and fluorescent light to 10 to 12 hours. Also lights were burned at night, to raise the temperature a little, and plants were in near darkness through the day. With this program, plants quickly resumed normal growth, although at a slower rate than if they had been provided with more warmth and light. This was all a compromise adapted to the basement conditions.

A man in San Francisco had a similar problem which appeared to be mite damage. In his basement setup, the temperature stayed between 70 and 75 degrees, the humidity nearly 70 percent, and lights were on for 14 to 16 hours. He changed his schedule, lowered humidity to 50 to 60 percent and burned lights for only 12 hours. Then he was able to grow African-violets with open centers and petioles of proper length.

If you are new at culture under lights, don't be discouraged when your plants fail to respond perfectly at the start. Almost everyone has to do a little experimenting. In the end, having achieved a satisfactory schedule, you will be greatly pleased—and so will your plants.

6

PUT DOWN A LEAF

*He who sees things grow from the beginning
will have the best view of them.*
Aristotle

Is there such a thing as one saintpaulia, just one? I doubt it, I have never known anybody to be satisfied with a single plant. It is usually obvious, even to an inexperienced eye, that every pot holds possibilities of more than one plant. In the beginning it's generally a matter of separating and repotting. Then the "secret of the leaf" is learned, and from there on, no limits are in sight. Indeed no, there can never be just one saintpaulia.

Probably no other plant offers four easier possibilities of increase. (1) You can divide plants with a multiple crown. (2) You can start new plants from suckers. (3) You can root leaves in soil or water. These are all "vegetative" methods involving green parts of the plant. (4) You can also grow a tremendous crop from one packet or one podful of seed, as I will disclose in the chapter that follows.

NEW PLANTS BY DIVISION

If you have a plant with more than one crown, you can with care separate it into a number of smaller individual plants. Let it dry out just a little before the operation. Dry soil and dry roots are easier to cope with than wet ones. Also, dry roots can be more readily pulled apart. First remove the plant from the pot. Then spread the plant out on a newspaper and gently but firmly pull the sections apart. Without any trouble at all you will get two or three single divisions.

76

The rest, a clump of two or three crowns, will probably cling stubbornly together. You can pot the whole thing and grow on a nice plant with a multiple crown, or take a chance, not always successful, and with a sharp knife cut it into single crowns. If you do any cutting, dust the parts with sulfur or Fermate so as to discourage unfriendly fungus organisms. Then grow all the divisions on the dry side; cuts will heal faster that way, and recovery be more likely.

Three-inch-diameter pots, or even 2¼'s are usually the right size for divisions with *some* root system. With plenty of surface room, plants soon develop their large handsome leaves to the fullest and maintain an open crown from which an almost constant procession of flowering stems will push forth. Use the same soil medium as before.

Suckers growing out at the sides of the crown are another source of new plants. Let them attain enough size to get hold of—and distinguish between them and an oncoming flower—before you cut them sharply away. Dust the cuts on parent and offspring with sulfur or Fermate; and on the sucker, use a very light dusting of a root stimulant such as Rootone. Then plant each sucker in a 2¼-inch pot, and grow it also a little on the dry side to discourage rot.

It is no trick at all to grow new plants from leaves (Figures 8 and 9). Select firm, medium-sized ones, preferably not from the last most mature "ring" of old leaves. (However, almost any leaf or part of one will grow; some growers even swear by the tiniest ones, which are more difficult to handle.) If an African-violet friend mails you a leaf and it looks wilted on arrival, soak the whole thing in tepid water for a few hours before you start it on its way.

Cut leaf stems (petioles) 1½ to 2 inches long. Trim the end on a slant or split up the center for about half an inch. There are two schools of thought here as to which method produces the most plantlets. In any case, cut with a sharp razor blade, and label each leaf with a strip of adhesive on which you have printed the name. Press the label onto the leaf surface. You could use plant labels, but the fastener sticker is safer.

Leaves rooted in water or in a mixture of three-fourths damp peatmoss and one-fourth vermiculite with a little fine-grade charcoal added or placed each in a separate pot with a central pocket of vermiculite surrounded by soil, develop into flowering-sized plants in about eight to nine months, very rarely in less time. However, the length of time depends on cultural conditions and also on the nature of the variety being propagated. Sometimes within a year, leaf-grown plants are large enough for division. So all you really need to satisfy even an unlimited enthusiasm for African-violets is a few leaves from plants of the varieties you admire, and, of course, considerable patience.

Many persons use horticultural-grade vermiculite alone, a mica product that comes by the bag and has the advantage of being already sterilized. The coarser particles may be included in the potting mixture, the finer used for rooting leaves, and the finest for planting seeds. If this vermiculite is pressed through a quarter-inch mesh screen, it readily separates into material of different degrees of coarseness. Most of those who have used this medium consider it a preventative of crown rot, and find that it aids the development of the plant. If you start leaves in vermiculite, try watering them every ten days with a *weak* solution of a soluble plant food.

ROOTING LEAVES IN WATER

Here are two practical methods developed for leaf propagation by home gardeners. Cover a water-filled glass tumbler with wax paper held in place with a rubber band; or aluminum foil can be crimped to stay by itself. Pierce the paper or foil in three places. Insert three leaf stems in these holes and deep enough for the stems to reach into the water. Set the glass in a fully light but not sunny window.

It is also possible to work even more simply. In a shallow glass dish or soup bowl a number of different varieties can easily be started. (This is the "community method.") Just fill the dish with enough small stones to support the leaf stems, and maintain a sufficient supply of water to keep the *ends* of the stems moist. If you have it, tuck bits of charcoal among the stones to keep the water fresh.

In two to four weeks, depending on variety and location, roots will appear. Change the water then unless you have used charcoal. By the end of another week or so a small green leaf may push out at the base of each parent leaf. If the parent leaf has begun to deteriorate, transfer the rooted leaves to a 2¼- or 3-inch pot of light soil or pure vermiculite and cut off the old leaf. If the parent leaf remains firm and healthy, wait until an inch-long cluster of leaves appears. Make the transfer from water to soil with all possible care, spooning the plantlet from aquatic to terrestrial life, and spreading the roots out gently in the soil mixture.

The time for rooting varies. No leaves can be depended upon to produce roots very promptly, but so long as the parent leaf remains healthy and does not soften and decay, the growth of roots and new leaves will eventually occur. Sometimes it actually takes months, but the spring of the year seems to be the most favorable time for setting leaf cuttings. They seem to grow with more vigor then while temperatures are cool, days neither hot nor cold, and the light stronger than in winter. The amount of growth also varies. The heavier growers like the Supremes send up fewer growth clusters (as they do flowers) than standard varieties which can be counted on for six or more new plants per leaf.

When quite a group of new leaves appears, cut the parent leaf away. Remove it sooner if it shows signs of deterioration, but often it is not necessary to discard it for a long time. If a variety is scarce or your supply limited, you may be able to grow a second or even a third crop from the same treasured leaf. Each time you will, of course, be working with a shorter, sharply cut petiole until a third planting is made perhaps with no petiole at all and only the leaf base to insert in the soil. Even so, you can expect success, for many have found that the same leaf will produce as fine a third crop as it did a first.

Expect some little setback at the time of the water-to-soil transfer while roots are adjusting to the new medium. In less than five months, however, you will have a well-established, thrifty plant that should, in less than a year, produce flowers.

ROOTING LEAVES IN SOIL OR A MIX

A second method has been developed by enthusiasts who prefer to start their plants in soil, a soil substitute like vermiculite, or in a favorite mixture like this one of Lucile Rainsberger's that has proved so successful for cuttings:

1 part coarse sand, sterilized
1 part peatmoss, sterilized
1 part vermiculite
½ part granulated charcoal (#7 or #10)

When cuttings have produced 1- to 1½-inch plantlets, they can be potted directly in two parts of this well mixed with one part of Nature's Way (Chapter 3) or they can be handled in this time-saving way worked out by Lucile Rainsberger: "Place drainage material in the bottom of each 2½-inch pot. Fill with the growing mix. Then scoop out a ¾-inch hole in the center and fill with damp vermiculite. Set the plantlet in the vermiculite and water with warm water. When the little plant takes hold in the vermiculite, its roots will grow right out into the nourishing soil mix."

FIGURES 8–9

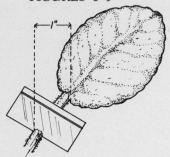

Use a sharp knife or razor blade to cut healthy leaves with inch-long petioles from the parent plant.

To root violet leaves in water, place foil or waxed paper over top of small glass or bottle. Insert leaves through holes in covering.

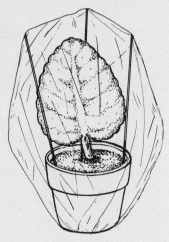

To root one violet leaf, use a 2¼-inch pot filled with sterilized potting soil (or other rooting medium such as vermiculite alone, or mixed in equal parts with peat-moss). Prop leaf in place with plant label. Cover with drinking glass, fruit jar, or clear plastic held up by small sticks (as shown).

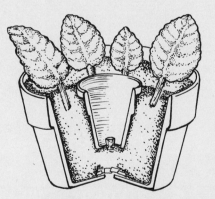

Leaves root readily in soil kept evenly moist by the pot-in-pan method. Small pot to hold water is porous clay with corked drainage hole. Larger pan may be of clay or plastic.

K. BOURKE

80

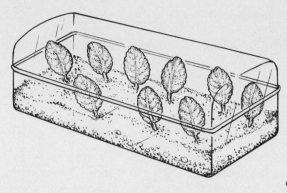

A plastic breadbox or unused aquarium can be turned into a miniature greenhouse for rooting violet leaves. The constantly moist atmosphere inside benefits newly transplanted seedlings or convalescent plants.

When leaf has formed a good system of roots in water, transplant with care to a small pot of soil; provide high humidity. When new leaves are a third as big as parent, young plants may be divided.

Plants at the 4½-to 5-months stage are ready to be planted in 2¼-inch pots. Separate tender plants and roots carefully. Blooms come in 6 to 12 months from time leaf is put down to root.

Experience indicates that battery jars, terrariums, and aquariums are excellent makeshift greenhouses for propagating, or even a pot or deep ashtray with a drinking glass inverted over it.

Over the bottom of a fish bowl or other suitable receptacle spread an inch of pebbles. Cover the small stones with a couple of inches of fine, sterilized, sandy soil, moistened but not made soggy. Then insert the leaves just deep enough for them to escape the soil surface. If they rest on it, decay may start. (If you have trouble making leaves stand up, prop them with toothpicks or plant labels.)

Firm the sandy soil mixture (or other rooting medium such as vermiculite alone or mixed half and half with peatmoss) well around each stem. Set the makeshift greenhouse in a light but not sunny place. If it has no top, stretch a piece of plastic over it, secured by a rubber band.

Little attention will now be needed for several weeks. The first few days after you plant, inspect the soil to be sure you moistened it well enough at the start for it to stay damp. If moisture collects on the sides of the glass, remove the cover long enough to wipe away the excess. In a not-too-warm and not sunny place such attention will hardly be necessary. In three to six weeks the rooted leaves will be at the new-plant stage and ready for separate potting. Some who have followed this plan, report bloom on new plants in six months.

POT-IN-PAN METHOD

Then there is the pot-in-pan method, as in Figure 8. Use moist sand (or perlite) and peatmoss, or vermiculite for a rooting medium. Fill a large clay bulb pan, or one made of plastic, with this and into the center insert a small corked-up porous clay flowerpot. Keep this small pot filled with water. The amount of water will decrease because of slow seepage through the walls of the inner pot. This seepage provides the surrounding soil area with adequate and even moisture. Insert the leaf stems in the rooting medium at a slight angle, the upper surfaces to the front. In two to four weeks roots will form. Once leaves have rooted, plants can be literally pushed along with proper feeding. A weekly dose of Liquid Blue Whale—½ teaspoon to 1 gallon tepid water—has proved an excellent booster, or weak biweekly feedings of Peters or some other soluble fertilizer, the half teaspoon dosage reduced to a quarter. In the course of another month, new sprouts will push up to the surface. In three months' time, well-developed plants will be ready for separate potting.

Any one of these methods—glass of water, aquarium or other make-shift greenhouse, pot-in-pan, or your own variation of them—will start a saintpaulia collection for you or increase the valued number of plants already in hand. Rooting and flowering seem to be hastened by a spring rather than an autumn start. There are a few reports of late September flowering from early May propagating. Perhaps the old idea that leaf-to-blossom took a year was based on autumn and winter propagating. Even so, flowering in less than eight to nine months is fairly unusual. Heredity and culture play a part in performance, and most certainly a humid atmosphere hastens bloom.

THE FASCINATING PROBLEMS OF VARIEGATION

Why African-violets develop variegated leaves and how to propo-gate variegations remain of major interest to all of us. The condition we see and refer to as variegation is of two kinds, one caused by certain environmental conditions, as soil deficiency or even pot bind-ing, the other, as in girl-type leaves, a true variegation that can be inherited.

When the colored areas on a leaf run into each other and are not sharply defined, plants are usually suffering from a soil deficiency, probably absence of iron or manganese or other trace elements essen-tial to the production of chlorophyll. Streaking in particular may indicate manganese deficiency. Restore balance to the soil and the "variegated" leaves may die or lose their variegation. It is even possible to starve or pot-bind a plant into greater variegation. Propagate leaves from such variegateds and all may be green, unless the rooting leaves suffer from the same deficiencies as the parent plants.

True variegation is a mutation. As such it can be transmitted to its seedlings, but genetically the matter is quite complicated. The ten-dency for streaking, as well as for areas of plain leaves (not girl types) to be partially or entirely white, will be seen in seedlings only if the variegated parent bears the seeds. Girl-type leaves, that is those with a distinct regular white or creamy chartreuse area at the base near the petiole, occurred first as a mutation among the plain-leaved plants of 'Blue Boy', our first famous named saintpaulia. The new variety was appropriately called 'Blue Girl'. We know today that the trait for girl-type foliage is dominant, regardless of which parent bears the seed.

It is interesting historically that one spring the people at Tinari Greenhouses put to root a row of S. *ionantha*—fifty to seventy-five leaf cuttings—and the plantlets on all of these cuttings, every one, were variegated. That same spring they noticed considerable variegation elsewhere in the greenhouses. The next spring there weren't six variegateds in all, a slight percentage. From this, it might be concluded that environment brought about variegation.

In true variegation, as distinguished from bleaching or mineral-deficient soil, the colored areas remain under the most favorable cultural conditions. The surest way to propagate variegation is to divide a variegated plant or to take suckers from it, and recently Peters has introduced a special fertilizer for plants with true variegation.

BRIEF GUIDANCE TO MORE PLANTS

1. Divisions. Separate plants with more than one crown or center of growth. Remove pot, gently pull apart, and plant divisions separately in as small pots as possible. Cut tight sections apart at your own risk. Rub cuts with sulfur or Fermate. Grow on the dry side at first.

2. Suckers or side growths. Cut off and pot separately in 2¼-inch pots. Rub cuts with sulfur or Fermate.

3. Leaves. Sharply cut off with 1½-inch stems. Root in water, vermiculite, perlite, or in a mixture of equal parts peatmoss and vermiculite, perlite, or sand.

4. Variegated foliage. All-white leaves seldom root, but those with some green (chlorophyll) produce interesting results. Leaf variegation caused by mineral-deficient soil, or some other lack, probably won't carry to new plants through propagation, but when variegation occurs as a natural mutation, new plants produced by vegetative propagation will have the trait and variegated plants can also be produced from seed.

7

GROWING FROM SEED

We cannot conceive of matter being formed of nothing;
since things require a seed to start from.
Lucretius

Whenever I think about seeds, I recall these lines. Few gardeners ever become so familiar with the seed-to-flower process that they are not always a little thrilled over what happens. For me seed sowing will always be an adventure.

To have the fun of growing African-violets from seed, it is not necessary to pollinate your own plants. Today you can purchase from commercial growers fine strains of seeds, even seed from specific crosses, perhaps of the varieties you particularly admire. You will find that you can have blooming-sized plants from the dust-fine seed quite as soon as from plants grown from putting down a leaf, sometimes sooner. It depends on the varieties involved and on the growing conditions.

MEDIUMS FOR SOWING

You can sow seeds in any one of several mediums and get good results. What is important is that the mixture you prepare should have water-holding capacity, yet be light and well drained. Well-worked garden soil, a little sphagnum, and a liberal quantity of sand will fill the requirements. Or you may prefer to combine half-and-half perlite and milled sphagnum, which is a popular mix. In any of the sterile mediums, it is necessary to feed even tiny seedlings every week with a

85

soluble fertilizer at about one-fourth the recommended strength for mature plants.

With mixtures including soil, it is wise to sterilize by baking; or in the greenhouse with a chemical to prevent damping off of seedlings and to banish insects.

POT, PAN, OR DISH

For seed sowing, use an ordinary flowerpot or shallow bulb pan with a sheet of glass or polyethylene bag for a cover; or sow in a glass baking dish or casserole that has a cover. The glass cover makes a pot or dish act as a miniature greenhouse that maintains an evenly moist condition, essential to germination and early growth. Arrange the crocking and drainage layer for pot or bulb pan just as you would for a plant. Then fill in the soil mixture, making it fine as fine. It's easy to sift the top inch of soil through a kitchen strainer—a little coarser than a tea strainer—if you are working with only a few pots.

If you use a covered dish, spread an inch layer of small stones or bits of charcoal over the bottom, as in Figure 10. Charcoal has the advantage of keeping the soil fresh. Let peatmoss soak up water overnight. Then drain and squeeze fairly dry before mixing with other ingredients. Spread the planting medium, 1½ to 2 inches deep, depending on the dish used, over the stones or charcoal. Then pat it smooth.

Sprinkle the seeds ever so lightly over the carefully prepared soil in pot or dish. After sowing, firm the soil gently; it is not necessary to cover with additional soil. Then put the sheet of glass or polyethylene bag, or glass cover in place and move the planting to a warm, bright place. If the temperature ranges from 75 to 85 degrees F., germination will usually start in 12 to 14 days, and continue over several weeks, or even for a period of months, depending on the varieties sown. Bottom heat often speeds up germination. Once it starts, keep seedlings out of direct sun but in a good light window, and as close to the glass as possible. Under fluorescent light, keep seedlings as close as 3 to 4 inches from the tubes. Good light means sturdy, vigorous growth.

Keep the growing medium *barely damp, but never wet*. If moisture collects on the glass, remove it for a few minutes, dry it, and then replace. Plantings in glass dishes must be watered from above. Use a fine mist as from an atomizer to moisten without flooding, or make a little hole in one corner of the planting and water through this. Since glass coverings prevent much evaporation, you will find very little

FIGURE 10

Glass casserole
used for germinating.
Cover the bottom with
charcoal, then fill in
with a half-and-half
mixture of vermiculite,
and peatmoss, soaked
in water overnight
and squeezed dry.

Useful transplanting
tools — a notched plant
label and a small fork.

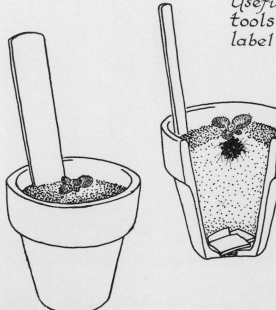

Seedlings appear
in about 3 weeks,
and are ready to
transplant when
they are ½ inch
high. Shift them
to 2- or 2½-inch
pots, in a mixture
of equal parts loam,
peatmoss, and sand,
or in a commer-
cially prepared
mixture.

Seeds and Seedlings

extra watering necessary. Water plantings in porous pots from below. Let them stand in water until the top soil is just moist.

SIGNS OF LIFE

In twelve to fourteen days, and continuing for perhaps four months, little green spears will appear. These will unfold cotyledons or seed leaves. When you see them, start watering about once a week with a mild solution of plant food. Hyponex or Ra-Pid-Gro is fine for this purpose. Mix at one-fourth the regular strength. Be watchful of damping off just after germination. If plants are too wet now, are in drafts, or get too little air, this rotting off due to fungus growth may start. If you see signs of trouble—mold or a cobwebby look—water right off with a fungicide, like Fermate, ¼ teaspoon to 2 cups of warm water.

Fermate mixes better if you do it like flour for gravy. First make a paste of the Fermate and a little water. Then add the rest of the water. It is also good to immerse leaf cuttings in before they are planted, or you can dip the ends in the dry powder, mixed half and half with talc. If small areas of rot occur on stems or leaves or leaf cuttings, apply a little dry Fermate with a small paintbrush to the affected parts. This may check the trouble.

When seedlings have three or four leaves and are about half an inch high, it is time for new quarters. Use a 2¼-inch pot for each, or set seedlings 2 inches apart in a flat or bulb pan. Avoid making seedlings compete for light, air, and nourishment. It's better to transplant over a long period than to wait to do the job all at once.

Move the largest youngsters the first day. If seedlings are allowed to stay too long where they started, petioles grow twisted and lengthy, the plant starts out spindly, and is unlikely ever to have a sturdy, healthy appearance.

Fill the small pots or flats for the seedlings with whatever soil mixture you have found successful for your larger plants. Be sure to sterilize whatever you use, unless it is a package of soil already sterilized by the concern that sold it. Just as soon as seedlings take hold and growth is obvious, apply weak liquid fertilizer at least once a week.

TRANSPLANTING

The first transplanting—four to six weeks after germination—is somewhat tedious. You don't want to move the seedlings "bare root." Each should carry along a tiny ball of the soil in which the seed germinated. A pickle fork seems the best tool to me (and at long last a use for this item), or you can just pry out each seedling by inserting a toothpick, nail file, or pen well down in the soil below it. Take along all the roots there are; don't break off a single strand (Figure 10).

Move your crop of potted seedlings into good light. A north window is usually a desirable location at this point. Seedlings won't want more than a glimpse of sun for another two months, or until they are well acclimated to growing alone. When they are established in the pots or flats—you will be able to tell from the way they start showing off with new leaves—you can move them to a location of filtered sunlight. Of course, seedlings of any age thrive under fluorescent lights, and somewhat closer to the tubes than you place mature plants, say 3 inches. Start *preventive* spraying with the pesticide you use on your other African-violets. Repeat as you do for mature plants, about once a month.

In six to nine months, the first exciting blooms may open. Promptness depends on varieties, season of the year, and growing conditions. Just think, at this point you don't even know what you are going to get! Exciting, isn't it?

BRIEF GUIDANCE ON SOWING

1. Prepare a light, moisture-holding mixture—soil, sand, and milled sphagnum moss or half-and-half perlite and sphagnum.

2. Use a flowerpot or bulb pan and cover with a sheet of glass or polyethylene bag; or sow in a casserole with a clear glass cover.

3. Sow on a moist soil surface—preferably, as soon as the pod is ripe—and press seeds down very lightly.

4. Put on cover.

5. Strive for a 75 to 85 degree F. temperature until after germination, then the usual 70 to 72 degrees.

6. Water just enough to maintain a barely moist condition, perhaps only once a week.

7. When the first green appears, start watering once a week, sparingly, with a weak fertilizer dissolved in tepid water.

8. In four to six weeks, before they are crowded, transplant to 2¼'s (pots), or to flats (space 2 inches apart) of your planting medium for mature African-violets.

9. Keep in a light place until two months after transplanting, or when new leaves indicate plants are well established. Then move to filtered sunshine. Seedlings of all ages thrive under fluorescent light culture. Set them 3 to 4 inches below.

10. Start monthly preventive spraying two weeks after transplanting.

11. Expect first flowers in six to twelve months under natural light. But under fluorescent lights, you may get bloom much earlier. Heredity plays a part and, as with leaf cuttings, good culture and particularly adequate humidity.

8

HOW TO HYBRIDIZE

The virtue of parents is a great dowry.
Horace

For the person who likes to start at the beginning, I have written this chapter. Some folks feel that growing plants from seed is the *only* way—and preferably from seed of their own pollinating. Otherwise they feel they see the show only after Act I is over. Certainly present-day African-violets have a complex ancestry and are so rich genetically as to promise a fascinating future. There will be varieties more beautiful than we can now envision.

One thing worries me when I tell what fun it is to cross your own saintpaulias. Will you exercise wisdom and be willing to keep only those new plants that actually surpass in some respect the varieties already in commerce? It may be true "there is no child like my child," but we must develop saintpaulia self-control. If, out of 500 seedlings, one is worthy of further cultivation, your efforts will not have been in vain.

WHAT IS YOUR GOAL?

We must recognize that in breeding saintpaulias there are two kinds of goals. One is the fun of doing, the other that fun plus the serious purpose of producing notably improved varieties. We must make a distinction. If we are only giving ourselves pleasant occupation, records will be less important, and so will results. We will also be most hesitant about naming, most hesitant. All those lovely seedlings, the majority of which are very like or perhaps duplicates of existing

91

varieties, we will just call Seedlings, and share them freely with friends and neighbors who will think of them as Mrs. Smith's African-violets or Uncle Bill's plants. Our venture then into cross-pollinating will have added to the sum total, never too great, of beauty and happiness in the world.

But suppose ours is a serious goal. We intend to develop new and better saintpaulias. Then we must prepare for a long discipline, sharpen considerably our critical faculties—and apply them to our own results. We must actually begin at the end and not the beginning, for we must determine today the goal we hope to achieve on a tomorrow that may be five years away.

What are the improvements most needed? Always better color— deeper, purer, and in new combinations. New flower shapes make saintpaulias more and more interesting. Remember when there were no star types? Now we are all thankful to the hybridizers who have nurtured this trait that gives us larger-than-ever African-violet flowers. Growers everywhere wait anxiously for new foliage shapes and patterns to emerge, at the same time hoping for smaller plants that flower abundantly. In this regard, Lyndon Lyon comments on the new German varieties which have particular appeal to florists: "Although some of our New World varieties far exceed them in flower size, range of color, and leaf types, hybridizers in this country will have to pay closer attention to developing free-blooming plants with long-lasting flowers on very strong stems." My own experience with them indicates a wealth of bloom but a thick type of growth that is quite difficult to reduce to a single crown. But plants need not all be models of flat shapeliness; these plants have other values, certainly brilliance of hue.

Perhaps your interest will lie in working with the miniatures. It isn't only the reduced space of modern living that makes these so appealing, for in their own right they have a very winsome charm. I never walk through the Plant Room without glancing at the special shelf some of my miniatures occupy.

Many of us are eager to obtain a free-flowering trailing African-violet, I particularly, because house-plant vines have always appealed to me more than upright growers. Of the pendent growers, Lyndon Lyon writes:

"The ideal trailing violet would really trail as much or more than the species S. *grotei*. Blossoms would be large with strong rather short stems and the leaves would be relatively small, the hanging effect would result from the rapidly elongating main stems. Flowers would be in all colors, forms, double and single stars, and there would be some wild type flowers. These trailers would make magnificent hanging baskets, pedestal plants, and big pot specimens, but some would be trailing miniatures with tiny leaves.

"Three and a half years ago, I started a long-range project to accomplish this. I wanted fast-growing trailers in a full range of sizes as well as colors, so early in 1966 I crossed S. *grotei* with 'Tiny Rose' and 'Tiny Pink'. In two generations I had pink star trailers, but about three fourths of the trailing characteristic was gone. I knew this would happen so I continued as I had planned. I selected the best of these and again crossed them on S. *grotei*. The resulting seedlings trailed much better than I expected, so to save time I crossed one of the best doubles on one of the best singles, and I have already potted sixty of the larger seedlings. I feel I am close to my goal, a rapid-trailing, vigorous pink star trailer that we can out-cross with to pick up new genetic traits and back-cross to, to again pick up the rapid-trailing characteristic in the full range of violet colors.

"I also have the species S. *magungensis minima* (a good trailer) which I have received in a shipment of twenty-five saintpaulia species from Henry Peterson. As Chairman of the Research Committee for the A. V. S. A., I hope to get a project started to test these and other varieties to find out how much variation there is in their tolerance to temperature and light with a view to breeding hardier varieties that will better survive and bloom in apartments, supermarkets, and florist shops."

ABOUT A YELLOW AFRICAN-VIOLET

We would all rejoice upon the announcement of an African-violet with yellow flowers—even a pale, but *clear* cream-yellow. But this seems to be an impossible dream unless a yellow-flowered saintpaulia species may still be discovered or a mutation occur that would give some yellow coloration. On this account, radiation has been used on African-violets, because it speeds up the mutation rate, and thus gives a better chance for yellow. But even with such artificial stimulation, mutations seem to be on the wane. Dr. Sheldon C. Reed remarks: "It is amazing how we had one mutation right after another fifteen years ago but since then there have been no new major mutations known to me."

The pigments which produce blue, purple, lavender, magenta, and pink colors in the African-violet are called anthocyanins. The pigments which produce orange and yellow flower colors are called anthoxanthins, xanthophills, and carotenoids. It is the anthoxanthins that are chemically closest to anthocyanins and through which a yellow-flowered saintpaulia just might come.

Of course, many persons are trying to cross closely related gesneriads that have yellow pigmentation with the saintpaulia. *Petrocosmea kerrii* is the leading candidate because of its white and yellow flowers. There are episcias with bright yellow flowers, but the likelihood that they will ever mate with saintpaulias is remote.

Breeders have been asked why they don't try crosses with the yellow violet of the outdoor garden. Such a mating would be as impossible as that of a black bird and canary to get a yellow black bird. The families are different. Violets are in the *Violaceae,* saintpaulias in the *Gesneriaceae.* I once overheard a lady say in all sincerity that she had been using pumpkin pollen on her saintpaulias in hopes of obtaining The Yellow!

We have all been so concerned about the yellow African-violet and about the modern roses that have no fragrance that very little thought has been given to the absence of fragrance in saintpaulias. It would be delightful if they had fragrance, but so far there has been no faintest whiff. None of the species have any and I know of no hybrid in existence which possesses this fine trait.

THE SCIENCE OF HEREDITY

To produce the improved saintpaulias of our dreams, a thorough working knowledge of genetics is needed. If there has been one benefit in *not* having a yellow saintpaulia, it has been the fact that in seeking it, all the African-violet world has become conscious of heredity. Many persons who recognize the great value of hybrid corn, hybrid tomatoes, hybrid fruits, are unaware that investigation of the same principles and subsequent work which gave us improved foodstuffs have also given us the superb roses, iris, lilacs, tulips, and countless other florist and garden plants we enjoy.

Apparently the double pinks constitute the first pioneer achievement of genetic knowledge applied to the field of African-violets. The doubleness of flowers (a Mendelian dominant) was combined with pink coloring (recessive in saintpaulias) to get the ancestors of the many marvelous double pinks we know today.

Those first double pinks were obtained by crossing a double purple with a single pink. Fifty percent of the seedlings turned out to be double purple, and there were no double pinks in this F_1 generation.

However, when one of those double purple seedlings was backcrossed on its single pink parent, twenty-five percent of the seedlings turned out to be double pinks. When we look back to the days when there were no pinks, much less *double* pinks, it is easy to see why many beginning hybridizers duplicate the cross outlined here, just for the satisfaction of recreating a historical step in saintpaulia improvement.

The science of heredity sets forth the basic laws by which we can predict how certain characteristics that we observe in a plant (or animal) will appear in its progeny, in what combinations and proportionate distribution. In other words, these are the rules that determine how resemblances and differences will be transmitted from parents to offspring—for not only one but many generations hence.

The laws of heredity were discovered by an Augustinian abbot, Gregor Mendel, in the 1860's. He worked with peas, growing them in the monastery garden in Brünn in Austria (now Brno, Czechoslovakia). His findings, published in 1866, were virtually ignored until 1900. Since then they have served to guide scientists to the extent that in the relatively few ensuing years we have made far greater improvements in plants and animals than had been made in the thousands of years before.

HYBRIDS AND CHROMOSOMES

Before we go further, let's clarify the meaning of the word "hybrid." A hybrid is the result of a cross between parents of different species, genera or varieties (the last two crosses sometimes defined as "crossbreed"). Apparently it is possible for two saintpaulia parents to resemble each other outwardly, but to carry entirely different genes that might produce worthwhile hybrids. The parents transmit their characteristics through the microscopic egg cell and tiny pollen grain. Progeny and parents are connected through the narrow hereditary bridge found in the chromosomes contained by the egg and the pollen grain.

The group of chemicals that makes up a chromosome forms a round or rod-shaped body. You can see this under a microscope. The exact arrangement of these chemicals within the chromosome is all-important. When it is spontaneously altered, we have a new kind of plant, and call it a mutant or sport. In every cell of every part—roots, stems, leaves, flower lobes—there are 30 chromosomes. Half of these came from the plant's father, and half came from its mother. Geneticists refer to the basic 15 chromosomes as *haploid,* and the two combined, or 30, as *diploid.*

Occasionally the number of chromosomes changes in a plant. The most common occurrence in saintpaulias is a change from 30 chromosomes to 60. The resulting plant is called a *tetraploid*. The Supreme strain of African-violets are tetraploids, recognizable by heavy-textured, brittle foliage and unusually large flowers.

A drug called colchicine is often used to induce African-violets (and other plants) to double their chromosome number. This material is placed on the base of the petiole a few days after it has been planted in the rooting medium. The colchicine prevents the usual cell wall from forming between two sets of 30 chromosomes, and with the 60 chromosomes locked together, the result is a tetraploid plant.

It would seem that the next step would be a doubled tetraploid, which would be an *octoploid* with 120 chromosomes per cell. To date this kind of plant has not occurred, but it is interesting to speculate about the way it would look. There are some excellent *triploids,* which result when a normal diploid (30 chromosomes) is crossed with a tetraploid (60 chromosomes). The resulting plants have 45 chromosomes, and have outstanding sturdiness and blooming qualities.

Chromosomes share the minute cell space with ingredients known as cytoplasm. Plastids, bodies within the cytoplasm, manufacture chlorophyll, the green substance found in plants. Without chlorophyll, plants would be unable to produce the sugars that they use for food. Plastids and other cytoplasmic materials are not inherited according to Mendel's laws. Instead they are carried from one generation to another only through the maternal parent. They cannot be carried from the father via the pollen grain. *This explains why plants with variegated foliage, usually showing a certain lack of chlorophyll, can pass this trait to seedlings only if the plant with variegated foliage acts as the mother, or seed-bearing parent.*

While cytoplasmic heredity is of interest, and value to the hybridizer, it is the chromosomal or Mendelian inheritance that is of vital importance, and through which the traits of flower color and leaf shape are carried.

LAW OF SEGREGATION

Mendel's first principle, the Law of Segregation, applies to African-violets in this way: If you cross African-violets of different shapes or colors, the hybrid seedlings that result will hold the heredity for these different traits inviolate in their cells. What goes in must come out. Colors, for example, that go into a cross will emerge again, that is segregate out in the next or later generations, and they do this in definite ratios.

This law is applicable to all living organisms. The most basic example we can make with African-violets is to cross two plants of 'Blue Boy'. Because this plant carries a gene for red flower color, one out of four seedlings will have red flowers. We say that the red gene is concealed by the dominant blue gene. This brings up another word, "dominant," in our discussion, and its meaning is obvious. The red gene is said to be "recessive" to the blue.

To illustrate dominance another way, consider a plant with boy-type leaves and one with girl-type, that is, with a white spot at the base where it joins the petiole. The gene for girl-type leaves is dominant to that which is responsible for boy-type. The chromosomes, with the genes they carry, occur in pairs. If one or both of these is a girl-type gene, then the seedlings will have girl-type foliage. Only when both genes carried by the chromosomes are boy-type will the foliage be plain. If you cross two plants with girl-type leaves, but both have the boy-type gene present, the seedlings will divide into a 3:1 ratio, with 75 percent showing girl-type foliage, 25 percent boy-type. Of the 100 percent total, 25 will have two girl genes, 50 will have one boy and one girl gene, and 25 will have two boy genes. This is the same 3:1 ratio demonstrated by crossing two plants of 'Blue Boy', both of which carry a recessive red gene.

The 1:1 ratio is also of interest. It is derived like this: The parent generation plants are designated as P_1. The offspring of the first generation are known as F_1, and if two first-generation plants are crossed with each other, the second generation seedlings will be known as F_2 hybrids. But, to back up, crossing an F_1 hybrid with its recessive P_1 generation parent will produce seedlings that give the 1:1 ratio.

The best illustration I know of this would utilize a plant with star-shaped flowers and one with plain flowers like those of 'Blue Boy'. When crossed, the F_1 generation would show no flowers with the star shape, since this is carried by a recessive gene. If however, one of these F_1 seedlings is backcrossed onto the parent with star-shaped flowers, the progeny will show about half with star-shaped flowers, half with plain ones—thus a 1:1 ratio. This illustration is hardly complete, however, without pointing out that when these F_1 seedlings are crossed with each other, the F_2 progeny will divide into a 3:1 ratio, with 25 percent of the plants showing perfect star-shaped flowers.

LAW OF INDEPENDENT ASSORTMENT

Mendel's Law of Independent Assortment is the next with which the saintpaulia hybridizer needs to familiarize himself. While Mendel's Law of Segregation has to do with only a single pair of genes, this second one deals with two or more pairs of genes, and sets down the fact that they work independently of each other. Here is a simple example, the most basic I can think of: If you cross a hybrid with boy-type leaves and double flowers with another hybrid having girl-type leaves and single flowers, the progeny would divide into fairly equal numbers of single-flowered girl-types, double-flowered girl-types, single-flowered boy-types, and double-flowered boy-types. Obviously we have obtained two 1:1 ratios—equal numbers of double flowers to single flowers, and equal numbers of girl-type to boy-type leaves.

This leads to the crossing of two plants with 3:1 ratios. Take, for example, a star-shaped purple flower and a plant with typical pink, African-violet-shaped flowers. Multiplying two 3:1 ratios obviously gives a 9:3:3:1 ratio, and several hybridizers have made a cross between the two types described above. The F_1 generation presents nothing of interest—only purple flowers of normal shape. If, however, two of the F_1 plants are crossed with each other, or one is selfed, the F_2 progeny will divide neatly into the 9:3:3:1 ratio. There will be nine with plain purple flowers, three with purple star-shaped flowers, three with pink standard-shaped flowers, and one with pink star-shaped flowers.

LAW OF LINKAGE

Morgan's Law of Linkage is another item of knowledge that the saintpaulia hybridizer needs. In a way it contradicts Mendel's Law of Independence Assortment, demonstrated earlier in this chapter. We know that the gene for double flowers occurs with its partner, the gene for single flowers. The chromosome that carries the gene for pink or not-pink is entirely separate from the pair of chromosomes that carries the genes for double and single flowers. However, it might be assumed that the gene for girl-type leaves would appear on still a third pair of chromosomes, but it does not. It is on the chromosome with the pink gene, or its partner, not-pink. Because the genes for pink and girl are located physically on the same chromosome, they are linked to each other. Consequently they are unable to sort out independent of each other in the progeny.

It is logical to ask how we ever got a plant with pink flowers and girl-type foliage. This occurred through a process called Crossing-over. This is possible because the chromosomes are long and cablelike and frequently lie across their partners. One of these may break and rejoin the other partner instead of the original. This is the way the gene for pink and the gene for girl got on the same chromosome. Thus 'Pink Girl' came into being and ushered in an important new era for African-violets.

AFRICAN-VIOLET ANATOMY

After learning the basic concepts of genetics, to work with pollination, you will need to understand the botanical elements involved in cross-fertilization (see Figure 11). The saintpaulia produces bisexual flowers, that is, each one contains both male and female organs. Study the drawings in this chapter. Then examine a flower and you will discover that besides the obvious five petals (really lobes), it has three other distinct parts.

The pair of small yellow sacs in the center holds the pollen or male fertilizing agent. These sacs are called anthers and are attached by short yellow filaments to the center of the flower. Anther and filament are the two parts of a stamen. You will see also another filament-like organ, longer, and quite prominent. This grows out at a sharp angle from close to the pollen sacs. It is the style, usually the same color as the petals. However, variegated-type blossoms may not conform as to color of the style. For instance, one white and orchid flower has an orchid style. Loosely, the style and stigma are usually called the "pistil," but are only part of it.

The actual entire pistil is the female element. Noticeably different from the stamens, it consists of three distinguishable parts. Low down at its base is a slight enlargement in which are held the immature seeds or ovules awaiting fertilization. This swelling elongates into the slender column called the style, which terminates in a tiny disklike structure known as the stigma. This becomes sticky after a flower has been open for a few days and continues so for several hours after petals fall. During this quite long interval in the plant's development, the stigma will retain grains of pollen on its surface if you (or an insect) transfer them there from an anther. Hand-pollination obviously refers to pollination by man.

At the base of the flower is a green enfolding structure composed of five sepals. These form a protective envelope, first for the developing

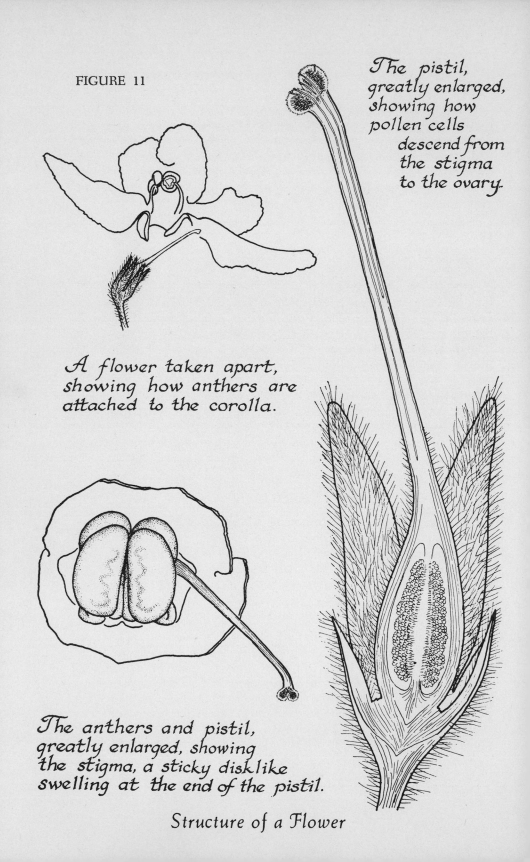

FIGURE 11

*The pistil,
greatly enlarged,
showing how
pollen cells
    descend from
    the stigma
    to the ovary.*

*A flower taken apart,
showing how anthers are
attached to the corolla.*

*The anthers and pistil,
greatly enlarged, showing
the stigma, a sticky disklike
swelling at the end of the pistil.*

Structure of a Flower

bud and later, after germination has occurred and petals have fallen, for the developing seed pod. Such a sensible arrangement!

Although each saintpaulia blossom does have these necessary male and female elements for self-fertilization, this does not commonly occur. Indeed, the way the pistil of each flower points away from the source of fertilizing pollen grains would seem to indicate an effort to avoid contact.

From window-sill gardeners and greenhouse people, there are reports of seed formation without hand-pollination. When a seed capsule forms indoors, it is possible that an ant or a house fly has been the pollen-carrying agent. In nature, it is also an insect or the wind that scatters pollen and brings it in touch with stigmas. However, those who have observed the saintpaulia in Tanganyika Territory (now the Republic of Tanzania), the natural habitat, report that even there, in the out-of-doors, there is but meager setting of seed.

With hand-pollination, seed is freely set. Look into the greenhouse of any hybridizer for example, and you will see mature plants each bearing many seed pods. If you examine the Supreme plants with capsules in early stages of development, you will notice that, as you expect, they are larger than those on other varieties, but examine ripe seed pods on these same plants and you will see, as you probably didn't expect, that they are just about the same size as those on the standard varieties (Figure 12).

HOW TO HAND-POLLINATE

Now just what is this method of pollination that results in the formation of seed pods? Pollination is a term describing the reception and retention of pollen by the stigma. When a cross "takes," the ovary or seed pod at the base of the pistil begins to enlarge and finally to project beyond the protecting sepals. It requires from six to nine months for seed to mature and ripen sufficiently for sowing. Spring pollination usually produces seed in about six months, while summer and autumn pollination requires eight to nine months.

Commercial growers in their pollination program usually start by removing, if possible, even before the bud opens, unwanted pollen-bearing anthers from the female parent, so as to avoid self-fertilization. Only occasionally will anthers burst and shed pollen naturally. As a rule, you have to open the small sacs, but to guard against the occasional burst, it is wise to remove pollen sacs from all seed parents. Use pollen from different plants of the same variety to reproduce, approxi-

FIGURE 12

Seed Pods of African Violets
showing widely varying shapes

mately, that variety. Use pollen from one variety on the stigma of another to get a hybrid. You can transfer the pollen from the anther of the chosen male parent to the stigma of the chosen female by one of several methods.

One way is to cut a tiny section in the yellow anthers of the selected male parent, let the pollen dust fall on your thumbnail, and then brush it over the disclike stigma of the selected female flower. The process could hardly be simpler. You may prefer to remove the anthers, carry them to the other parent, and insert the stigma into the snipped pollen sacs, or to transfer pollen by means of a small paintbrush. By whatever method, the end result should be stigmas yellow with pollen grains (Figure 13).

The best stage for pollinating is when a flower appears mature—not old, not newly open, but fully developed. You will have to observe your plants closely, and experiment a little to determine the best time for collecting pollen. It has long viability. There is evidence that pollen mailed great distances has still produced successful crosses, and that a year's proper storage does not destroy it:

When the pollen grain comes in contact with the stigma, fertilization does not immediately take place. First the protoplasm around the pollen cells elongates. It bores down through the style (which supports the stigma), forming a pollen tube. The male elements within the tube advance as the tube elongates, until the tube enters the ovule. Then the chromosomes are released and join with those of the ovules or eggs in the ovary, and fertilization has occurred.

Fertilized plants should be tagged so as to have an easy, readable record always at hand. Small string tags with the name of the cross as Seed Parent X Pollen Parent are useful. A numbered record is shown at the end of this chapter. An actual record should be kept for each cross, if in the end you want to know what you have and how it has behaved.

SEED PLANTS AND THE CROP

Growers should keep the plants that are producing seed somewhat on the dry side, and insure a better than usual circulation of air. Examine daily for rotted petioles. These could start softening of the pedicels bearing seed pods. A close atmosphere may result in the softening of seed pods before they are mature. If this occurs, snip them off, and spread them out in a warm dry place. So treated they may mature even though away from the plant. There is disagreement

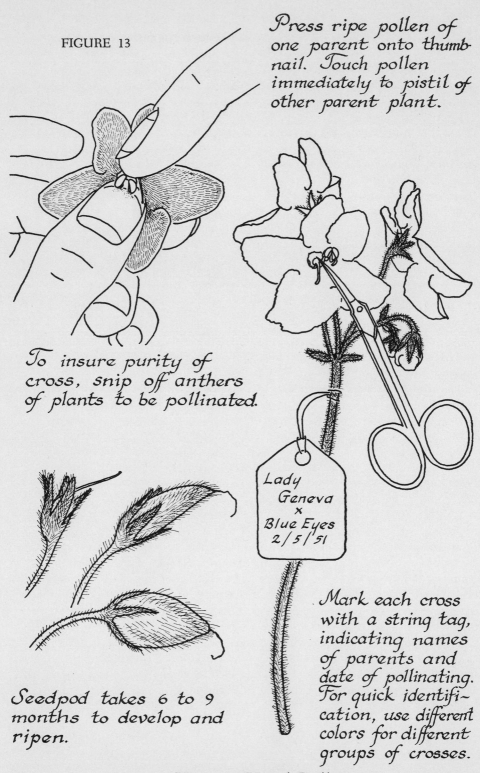

FIGURE 13

Press ripe pollen of one parent onto thumb-nail. Touch pollen immediately to pistil of other parent plant.

To insure purity of cross, snip off anthers of plants to be pollinated.

Lady Geneva x Blue Eyes 2/5/51

Seedpod takes 6 to 9 months to develop and ripen.

Mark each cross with a string tag, indicating names of parents and date of pollinating. For quick identification, use different colors for different groups of crosses.

How to Hand-Pollinate

as to whether it it necessary to remove flowers from plants with developing seed pods. I think the seeding is more likely to detract from the flowering than vice versa.

Completely developed seed pods shrivel, dry, and turn brown on the plant. When they look "done," remove them, with the flower stalk attached. The usual practice is to let the capsules dry for a month to six weeks, but you can plant at once, or you can wait for as long as a year. The vitality of these tiny seeds is amazing. Some varieties germinate very unevenly. I find that seeds from one pod may start to germinate in a couple of weeks and continue to do so for four months.

When the pods are dried, split them open and sow the seeds, or store the pods until you are ready in labeled envelopes, small jars, or well-capped plastic bottles from your pharmacist. Keep the stored seeds in a slightly cool place. A temperature of 60 to 65 degrees F. is fine.

Now what can you expect from the seeds of your carefully made crosses? Just about anything. If you are familiar with Mendel's laws you may be looking for a certain number of the offspring to resemble one parent, a certain number the other, and some to combine the parents' characteristics, both the dominant and the recessive ones. Keep in mind, however, that with the exception of the species, you are working with plants of complex genetic makeup that offer infinite possibilities. Actually every cross represents a small miracle, and who is not filled with awe at this intimate revelation of Nature's manifold designs?

Most hybridizers bring seedlings to flower in 2¼-inch pots. At first flowering, if a seedling shows no valuable trait, it is discarded immediately, always to give space to something better. As a hybridizer, you will need some kind of system for measuring seedlings. This might include, (1) vertical and horizontal dimensions of the flower, (2) length of stem, (3) length and width of the leaf, (4) length of the leaf stalk (or petiole), (5) number of flowers and buds per stem, and (6) number of flower stems on the plant. At this time, if flower size is commendable, or coloration is an improvement, or there is something definitely good about the plant, it probably deserves a 3- or 4-inch pot, unless of course you are working with a miniature.

If yours has been a serious effort, perhaps a project involving considerable expense, you will examine your developing plants and the first flowers with concern, if not anxiety. Do I have anything? you will ask, meaning anything promising for introduction. If you decide you have, propagate it *vegetatively* two or three times (hybrids do not come true from seed). You would also do well to self-fertilize a few plants to see what the seedlings are like. Perhaps you have an important mutant (which does come true from seed), and not a hybrid at all.

HOW TO REGISTER NEW VARIETIES

The next question must be, is it worth registering? If your plants are as good as or almost the same as acknowledged varieties, even the best of them, please do not register. So much near duplication and exact duplication already exists that it is too bad to increase nomenclature problems. If something really better, a better strain, for instance, or something undoubtedly new appears, by all means plan to develop as much stock for introduction as you can.

But first take steps to give status to what you think is a new variety. Write to Registrar, AVSA, Inc., Mrs. Fred Tretter, 4988 Schollmeyer Ave., St. Louis, Missouri, 63109, and request the number of Registration Cards you need, two for each variety. Study the cards and either type or print clearly all requested information on one card for each variety. Make a duplicate for your files. Be sure to give all needed information as this is the only record of your plant and the Registrar will not accept Registrations that do not contain the required data. Send your completed cards plus a fee of $3.00 for each variety to be registered to the Registrar. The cards are quite simple and easy to fill out.

There is a possibility that your variety will be contested. The name may already have been used, or another grower may have established a prior claim, or someone else may have produced the same variety you have. Don't feel too bad if this happens.

Scientific discoveries, to which men have devoted their lives, have been simultaneously announced, even in distant quarters of the globe. If your variety is challenged in writing, as is required, the decision rests with the AVSA Registration Committee. All this is fair and square and, as an ardent saintpaulia fan, you will undoubtedly be grateful for this means of giving your variety legal status, or if it does not deserve it, of being saved from compounding present confusion.

Sample Record of a Cross

#11   Name of seed parent X name of pollen parent
3/1   Cross-pollinated plant
3/14   Signs cross has taken

10/5   Seed pod looked mushy. Removed with a long stem, placed in a small dish in the china closet. Kept at room temperature.

1/4   Sowed seeds in two-thirds sterilized peatmoss, one-third vermiculite.

1/22   Germination just visible

1/30   Watered with warm Hyponex water (¼ teaspoonful to 1 quart of water).

2/7   Hyponex again. (Could have used any other well-known brand, such as Plant Marvel or Ra-Pid-Gro with equal success.)

3/20   Transplanted largest seedlings to covered dish (continued transplanting until 6/15).

5/15   Transplanted first seedlings to 2¼'s in soil mixture.

7/28   First flower. Medium blue resembling seed parent. Other seedlings showing buds.

12/10 F_2. Selfed the selected seedling—a nice dark blue. (Leaf cuttings from this seedling reproduced true through three vegetative reproductions, which took time.)

10/1 F_3. Seeds planted

Results: A dark seedling apparently a better dark blue Supreme than present one—improved foliage and fatter blossom of good substance and fine color. No name yet.

Brief Guidance to Pollination

1. Select parents each with some outstanding characteristic—perhaps take pollen from a parent with fine flowers and select a seed parent for quality foliage.
2. Pollinate, preferably toward spring, but anytime under fluorescent lights. Be sure the stigma is sticky.
3. Snip open pollen sacs of selected male parent with a manicure scissors, and let pollen fall on your thumbnail.
4. Rub pollen on stigma of selected female parent.
5. In 7 to 14 days look for swelling of ovaries.
6. In 6 weeks, expect well-developed pods or capsules extending beyond sepals.
7. In 6 to 9 months remove seed pods, as dried, shriveled condition indicates maturity.
8. Let pods dry in a warm place for 4 to 6 weeks after gathering, or sow seed at once.

9

THE FASCINATING
SPECIES

Let us a little permit Nature to take her way;
she better understands her own affairs than we.
Montaigne

It was in 1892 that the African-violet was discovered in "the hilly regions of Eastern tropical Africa," and the next year it flowered for the first time in Europe, thousands of miles from its habitat. From the day of its discovery, the saintpaulia took the horticultural world by storm. An important garden magazine of the time noted, beside the drawing reproduced in Figure 1: "It does not often happen that a plant newly introduced into Europe can claim the honor accorded to the subject of this plate, of being within two years of its flowering figured in five first-class horticultural periodicals."

The African-violet or Usambara-violet, as it is also called, belongs to the Gesneriad family, and holds no kinship to any true violet. Even so, "African-violet" seems an appropriate name when we consider the plant's origin, and its flower suggesting a violet in color and form. The related gesneriads, described in Chapter 15, yield a storehouse of other interesting plants from which the indoor gardener may choose.

The African-violet was first found by Baron Walter von Saint Paul, the Imperial District Captain of Usambara, a province of northeast

Tanganyika in the Territory of East Africa. He sent either plants or, more likely, seeds of "das violette Usambara" to his father, Hofs-marschal Baron von Saint Paul of Fischback in Silesia. The father was, fortunately for us, a man keenly interested in plants, especially trees—in fact he was president of the Dendrological Society of Germany.

To the publisher of *Curtis's Botanical Magazine,* that enchanting English periodical which you can perhaps find in bound volumes in a fine horticultural library, he wrote:

"The *Saintpaulia* was discovered by my son, who lives in East Africa where he owns planatations of vanilla [vines] and India-rubber trees. It was found in two localities; one about an hour from Tanga, in wooded places, in the fissures of limestone rocks, as well as rich soil with plenty of vegetable matter. This place is not more than 50 to 150 feet above the sea level. The second place is in the primeval forest of Numbara, likewise in shady situations, but no granite rocks, 2500 feet above the sea. It is much more plentiful in the former place. Several varieties have been discovered that differ slightly in color of the flowers but all are blue."

The Hofsmarschal took plants to Herman Wendland, Director of the Royal Botanical Gardens at Herrenhausen. It was the Director who named the plant for the Saint Paul family, described it in Latin, and gave it the species name, *ionantha,* "with violet-like flowers." He exhibited flowering plants in Ghent at the International Horticultural Exhibit, where they "shared with Eulophiella exhibited by Messrs. Linden the honour of being the two most botanically interesting plants in the exhibition."

The next year continental nurserymen carried the seed; and the *Revue l'Horticulture Belge Etrangère,* beside a picture of a rather unrealistic and very blue saintpaulia with very pink petal reverses, remarked, "*Sa floraison est ininterrompue pendant tout l'hiver. . . . Elle sera promptement accueillie par tous les amateurs auxquels elle promet les plus vives jouissances aux époques de l'année où les fleurs sont les plus rares.*" And plants of this marvelous subject blooming "in the time of year when flowers are rarest" were offered by L'Etablisse-ment Ed. Pynaert-Van Geert for six francs each. Flowering plants were also developed in the Royal Gardens of England.

The first commercial plantsman to see the possibilities of our saint-paulia and offer it to the world was Friedrich Benary of the seed house of Ernst Benary of Erfurt, Germany. Evidently the firm received rights in 1893, and seed production and distribution were started. A red-violet variety was announced in 1898. Then *alba,* a white, and various others, as *atrocoerulea* and *purpurea.*

At the outset, Mr. Benary made certain interesting observations on the new plant he was handling, "It seems to be quite a peculiarity of this plant to produce capsules of two different shapes . . . one long and the other round-shaped." He added that the different types of capsule were never found on the same plant. It is now concluded that the short-fruited plants were specimens of S. *ionantha.* Seed pods are shown in Figure 12.

In recent years Mr. B. L. Burtt formerly of the Herbarium at Kew, now at the Royal Botanic Garden at Edinburgh, has designated the long-fruited plants as S. *confusa.* These have a "dual indumentum of long and short hairs which clothe the leaves, contrasting with the hairs of uniform length found on S. *ionantha.*" When I talked with Mr. Burtt in England in 1949, he predicted that further investigation was going to reveal a number of species. Already he had noted S. *tongwensis* and S. *orbicularis.*

Meanwhile in this country research had been undertaken by Evan Paul Roberts and Harvey Cox. Their fascinating articles have appeared regularly since March, 1950, in the *African Violet Magazine.* All of us interested in the past of the saintpaulia, as well as its lovely present and marvelously unpredictable future, have enjoyed the reports.

The species are not so colorful as the hybrids but you may find a special delight in making a collection of these originals. Plant breeders also find them useful. Our present African-violets are probably descendants of S. *ionantha* and S. *confusa.* A variety that tends to creep, cascade, or climb may have S. *grotei* or some other trailing species in its ancestry.

The species descriptions that follow are based mainly on the Roberts-Cox reports, as well as on a paper prepared in 1958 by Mr. Burtt and published as a supplement to the *African Violet Magazine* in March, 1960. The flowers of all species known to date are single.

SAINTPAULIA AMANIENSIS

The plant was discovered in the foothills of the Usambara Mountains near Amani and appears to be related to S. *magungensis,* S. *grotei,* and S. *goetzeana,* all of which have creeping stems. The violet-blue flowers with deeper centers come in pairs or clusters of four or five and measure about 1 inch across. Leaves are medium green above,

Upper left, *Saintpaulia amaniensis*. Upper right, *S. confusa*. Lower left, *S. difficilis*. USDA photos. Lower right, *S. goetzeana*. *African Violet Magazine* photo.

pale greenish white below, ovate to ovate-elliptical, 1 to 2 inches long and ⅞ to 1½ inches wide. Margins are "crenate-dentate, slightly revolute" with midrib prominent. Petioles are 1½ to 3½ inches long, "stems procumbent-branched, rooting where they come in contact with soil, pale green, up to 10 cm. long." Vegetative parts are covered with long and short hairs intermixed. (*S. amaniensis* differs from *S. magungensis* in having oval-pointed rather than rounded leaves, but according to Mr. Burtt a thorough study has firmly established that S.

amaniensis is not a separate species but simply a form of *S. magungensis.*) It is, however, often listed as a species.

Saintpaulia amaniensis, as we know it, often grows as a multiple-crowned plant, and will trail from a shelf. It likes moisture and coolness with a little less light than the hybrids.

S. CONFUSA

This species was found on November 26, 1895, at altitudes of 1000 to 3000 feet on gneiss rock in the region of sacred Mt. Mlinga. The locale is fifteen miles north of Mt. Tongwe, the home of *S. tongwensis,* in the eastern Usambara Mountains. *S. confusa's* habitat is more moist than that of *S. tongwensis,* and in cultivation, *S. confusa* has shown need for more water. This is the other of those two species that Ernst Benary grew but did not distinguish, except to note that his plants bore different kinds of seed capsules. We know the round ones belong to *S. ionantha,* the long ones to *S. confusa,* which has been erroneously identified as *S. kewensis,* then as *S. diplotricha.*

Saintpaulia confusa blooms prolifically, though not as frequently as some species, producing clusters of two to five deep violet flowers, 1 inch across, and well above the foliage. The leaf is medium to light green, with slightly serrate margins, very smooth, slightly quilted, flat, and measuring 1⅝ to 2 inches. The petiole is thin, about 2 inches long.

The plants described by the African Violet Society in their first records were almost miniature, flat, of light rosette growth. Our photograph shows such a dwarf grower. This was easily propagated and tended to sucker freely. It now appears that if allowed to produce multiple crowns, *S. confusa* will develop into a very large and more attractive plant. It does well in a vertical position as on a moss totem or in a strawberry jar.

S. DIFFICILIS

Collected in the borderland of Kenya and Tanganyika by Dr. P. J. Greenway in 1939, this produces an upright, single crown with long leaf-stalks. This has been found in three places in the same general area; on rocks by a stream; in the evergreen Parinari dry forest valley; and on damp rocks in an evergreen rain forest. The pointed chartreuse leaves are distinctly veined, and they have a tendency to spoon. The flowers are of average size, medium to deep blue, profusely borne.

S. DIPLOTRICHA

This species from the eastern Usambara Mountains has thick deep green leaves, paler reverses, and very pale lilac flowers. It is often mistaken for S. confusa. Harold E. Moore, Jr., in *African Violets, Gloxinias, and Their Relatives* states: "It [S. diplotricha] may be distinguished from the similar S. confusa by the thicker purplish leaves which have the long hairs spreading and the short hairs erect in a rather dense but inconspicuous covering. This difference is most easily seen if the leaf is cut crosswise and viewed along the cut edge." The plant is small, growing in a flat rosette with a single crown.

S. GOETZEANA

This species was found by W. Goetze on large boulders among moss in the primeval forest of the central part of Uluguru on the south side of the Lukwangule plateau. The discoverer sent a good herbarium specimen to Professor Adolph Engler in Berlin, who published a description of it in his *Botanische Jahrbücher* on July 13, 1900. A small plant, S. goetzeana is not easily grown. It forms many rosettes of dark, ovate leaves that rise from a creeping stem; it looks like a pincushion. The flowers are pale lilac, nearly white, usually in clusters of three, but there is no record of their blooming in this country. The plants have very shallow roots.

S. GRANDIFOLIA

An excellent species, this was discovered by W. R. Punter in the western Usambara Mountains. There he found the plants growing in a steep valley on clay; S. grandifolia forms a single crown of medium ovate leaves which are thin textured, almost satiny, and of a clear green color. The dark violet flowers appear in large clusters, making this a showy species. It is sometimes called S. lutinde. It makes a fine large single-crown plant.

S. GROTEI

Discovered "in the vicinity of Amani, Tanganyika Territory, at an altitude of 3000 feet . . . in dense shade near running water . . . roots not submerged but located where drainage is perfect," S. grotei was first described in 1921 by Professor A. Engler of Berlin. Present-day plants, with benefit of greenhouse, produce larger flowers than those of the Professor's description.

Above, S. grandifolia. African Violet Magazine photo. Left, S. intermedia. USDA photo. Below, S. grotei. African Violet Magazine photo.

The flowers, in clusters of two or three, are bright blue-violet near the tips of the petals, shading darker toward the center. Apparently bloom is more frequent in warm weather. Seed pods measure more than an inch. The rounded, dentate leaf is medium green, almost flat, measuring 1 to 3½ inches. Sometimes small pockets or depressions appear between veins. The long, brown, leaf stems are the most obvious characteristic of S. grotei. On occasion these produce roots at the nodes, which are those small swellings you see on the stems.

Long stems to 3 feet or more make it possible for anyone to develop a cascade or hanging plant with S. grotei, or a climber if support is provided. The plant breeder has been discovering in S. grotei various stimulating possibilities.

S. INCONSPICUA

This species was first recorded in December, 1932, and in more detail two years later by E. M. Bruce who found it occurring only occasionally in the moist soil of a forest in the Uluguru Mountains of Morogoro on the Kisaki Road in Tanganyika. It has white flowers with a blue spot, quite small, and not typical of other African-violets. Perhaps this is one reason that S. inconspicua was first classified as a species of Didymocarpus, although taxonomists declare now that it is definitely a saintpaulia. The plant is of trailing habit. Apparently it is not in cultivation in this country. It sounds nice and perhaps will later be available to us.

S. INTERMEDIA

An interesting species, discovered by W. R. Punter, growing on rock at Kigongoi in the eastern Usambara Mountains, this is intermediate between rosette-forming saintpaulias and those that trail, like S. grotei. It often grows upright, as a single- or multiple-crowned plant. The leaves are almost round with finely serrated edges, pleasing olive-green color, and they have a tendency to spoon. The blue flowers appear in clusters of 5 or 6, in moderate numbers with no special coaxing needed.

S. IONANTHA

This was one of the original two species, but not then recognized as two, discovered by Baron von Saint Paul. Saintpaulia ionantha and S. confusa appear to be the ancestors of the hundreds of present-day varieties. Our drawing of S. ionantha, Figure 1, from Curtis's Botani-

Upper left, *Saintpaulia ionantha*. Upper right. S. *magungensis*. Lower left,
S. *nitida*. Lower right, S. *orbicularis*. USDA photos.

cal Magazine looks much like the S. *ionantha* we know today, as in Figure 2.

Saintpaulia ionantha produces light to dark blue-violet clusters of three to ten flowers, each about 1½ inches in diameter. The slightly pointed leaves are dark green, glossy, quilted, with slightly serrated margins and cordate bases. Leaves cup upward slightly and measure 2½ wide by 3½ inches long. The plant grows large and upright with somewhat drooping lower leaves. The heat tolerance of today's varieties is doubtless due to S. *ionantha* inheritance, since the average temperature of its native home is 80 degrees F.

S. MAGUNGENSIS

This more recently discovered species, first described by Mr. Roberts, in the *African Violet Magazine* for June, 1950, may be extinct in East Africa since a planting of sisal now covers the area whence it came. It was collected at Magunga in the foothills of the Usambara Mountains, and appears to be closely related to S. *grotei,* also from those mountains.

The flowers, in clusters of two to four, are medium violet-blue shading to a darker center, and the plant is a fairly good bloomer. The rounded leaves with crenate margins, cupped under a little, are medium green above and pale greenish white below, with midribs prominent. The petioles are 1¼ to 2¾ inches long. The stems are "procumbent, branched, rooting where they come in contact with soil, pale greenish when young and developing a brownish corky outer layer when older, 2½ to 5½ inches long." The vegetative parts of the plant are covered with long and short hairs, intermixed.

Mr. Roberts notes that S. *magungensis* differs from S. *grotei* "in having much smaller leaves, shorter petioles, crenate rather than dentate-crenate leaf margins, nonglandular hairs on margin of corolla, unlobed stigma, and darker flower color. All three of these procumbent species, like S. *confusa,* have a pubescence composed of hairs of two different lengths, intermixed.

"S. *magungensis* with its creeping, branching stems and its beautiful leaves cupping downward is indeed a valuable addition to the genus. It has an artistic habit of growing over the sides of the container . . . Possible future hybrids of it will undoubtedly have other colors . . . One of its hybrids has already developed into one of the most erect African-violet plants in existence in spite of the fact that S. *magungensis* is a creeping type . . . with branching stems. The possibilities are numerous." A miniature form has recently been found in a group of cultivated plants.

S. NITIDA

This dark-leaved species was found in the Nguru Mountains of Tanganyika, near Twiani, growing on rocks in shade by a forest stream. The small, shiny, round leaves are flexible, on slender brown or purplish petioles. *S. nitida* may be grown as an upright single-crowned specimen, although it tends to spread. It has dark blue-violet flowers in clusters.

S. ORBICULARIS

It was February, 1916, when this species was first discovered in the western Usambara Mountains between Sakarre and Ambangula. Mrs. R. E. Moreau rediscovered it in the same area in August, 1938. It was growing at an altitude of 4000 feet where, even in the shade, daytime temperatures reach well beyond 90 degrees F. Nighttime temperatures in June, July, and August drop to near 45 degrees F. *Saintpaulia orbicularis* was also found in the same mountains at Shume where the altitude is between 6000 and 7000 feet.

This handsome plant grows upright naturally with multiple crowns, but it can be grown to a single crown. Dark green shiny leaves, sometimes cupped, are small and nearly round to heart-shaped, on long, thin purplish-brown petioles. The small, light lilac flowers are dark-centered, and they appear abundantly in clusters held well above the foliage.

S. PENDULA

This caulescent species from Mt. Mtai in the eastern Usambara Mountains in Tanganyika has almost round leaves, gray-green, rather heavy-textured, with slighty serrate edges. Flowers are medium lavender blue, solitary or in two's, and 1¼ inches across. The plant is of trailing habit with multiple crowns.

S. PUSILLA

Also found by W. Goetz in the central Uluguru Mountains and described by Professor Engler in his *Botanische Jahrbücher* is this true miniature, measuring but 5 inches across, and so of inestimable value to breeders interested in developing small types. *Saintpaulia*

Upper left, *Saintpaulia pendula*. Upper right, *S. shumensis*. *African Violet Magazine* photos. Lower left, S. *tongwensis*. Lower right, S. *velutina*. USDA photos.

pusilla may still be found growing on large boulders among moss "in the primeval forests of the central Uluguru mountains, on the south side of the Lukwangule plateaus, 1200 to 1800 meters."

The tiny flowers are bicolored, light blue and white, and the petals "narrowly triangular." The capsule is elongated at the base. The small leaves are obtuse at both ends and purple beneath.

S. SHUMENSIS

This delightful miniature species produces many crowns set with small, nearly round leaves on short petioles. It comes from Shume in the western Usambara Mountains where it grows in dry forest on cliff faces. Be careful about giving it too much water. The clustered flowers are quite small, nearly white, with a deep violet spot in the center. It can be grown as a single-crown plant, but is a shy bloomer. Hybrids of other species with S. *shumensis* are not miniatures but of standard size.

S. TEITENSIS

Discovered in the autumn of 1938 by Boy Joanna in the Teita Hills, Mbololo Hill, Kenya, this species grew in the forest near water. The glossy dark green leaves may or may not have reddish purple reverses, and they occur on a long, unbranched stalk. To date this is the northernmost species known. The flowers are medium violet-blue with a darker center.

S. TONGWENSIS

This species was discovered at an altitude of 2300 feet on a 50-yard ledge of rock on the ridge of Mt. Tongwe. The area was surrounded by a barrier of 5-foot grass that evidently kept S. *tongwensis* "pure." It has not been distributed nor have seeds of other species penetrated the grass to effect crosses. H. B. Herring discovered the plant "growing in humus on gneiss rocks beneath a light shade of undergrowth." (Mr. Burtt described S. *tongwensis* in 1947.) In cultivation it blooms more freely at 80 to 90 degrees F. than at 65 to 75 degrees, although it blooms satisfactorily in the cooler range.

The flowers, 1⅛ inches across, in clusters of ten to twelve, are light blue. Plants bloom freely with plenty of space between flower stems. *Saintpaulia tongwensis* may be grown as a single-crowned plant. It does well in a semivertical position and makes a good subject for the moss totem or strawberry jar.

The leaf is rather transparent, heart-shaped, and dentate, measuring 2 by 3¼ inches. Multicellular hairs appear on older ones. There is a broad pale band along the center, running parallel to the midrib. This characteristic is particularly noticeable under artificial light. Petioles grow to 3½ inches and have spreading hairs. Seed pods are cylindrical,

Upper left, *Saintpaulia diplotricha*. USDA photo. Lower left, S. *shumensis* x S. *ionantha*. Below, S. *nitida* x S. *shumensis*. The two hybrids of S. *shumensis* are of average African-violet size. *African Violet Magazine* photos.

½ to ¾ of an inch long. The pale blue tint of S. *tongwensis* and the banded leaf are of interest to the breeder, and the plant is not difficult to grow.

S. VELUTINA

This species, sometimes listed as S. *coxiensis*, was first discovered by A. Peter in 1916. It is from the western Usambara Mountains, near Balangai, 5 miles from Sakarre. The upper leaf surfaces have a velvety appearance, contrasting with reddish reverses and petioles. The leaves are scalloped and heart-shaped, with interesting veining. The pale blue flowers with darker centers appear in abundance, but the plant resents heavy watering. It is characteristic for the lobes of S. *velutina* flowers to be white-tipped, and the species has a tendency to produce flowers with four fertile stamens instead of the usual two.

10

THE OLD FAVORITES

Old Friends burn dim, like lamps in noisome air;
Love them for what they are; nor love them less
Because to thee they are not what they were.
Coleridge

George Stumpp, a New York florist, was the first American to bring African-violets back from Germany very soon after the firm of Ernst Benary at Erfurt had offered them. About 1894 two of these plants came into the hands of William K. Harris, a Philadelphia florist, who propagated and made them available to his customers. For those little green pioneers living was a difficult thing in the Gay Nineties. Without the heating controls which we take for granted today, wintertime found the plants too hot or too cold; most of them were chilled unmercifully. Fortunately, while we were learning better heating methods, commercial growers in Europe who operated warm or "stove" houses continued to cultivate saintpaulias.

By 1927, when the first hybrid saintpaulia seeds came into this country, central heating had been vastly improved. Those first seeds became an important part of saintpaulia history, for they brought a new era for indoor gardeners, first in the United States, and ultimately throughout the world. Walter L. Armacost of Armacost & Royston, a California firm, obtained the seeds from Ernst Benary, the German grower, and from Sutton's in England. About a thousand seedlings were brought to maturity, and through several years' selectivity, ten outstanding plants were chosen and named. They were introduced in 1936 as 'Blue Boy', 'Sailor Boy', 'Admiral', 'Amethyst',

'Norseman', 'Neptune', 'Viking', 'Commodore', 'No. 32', and 'Mermaid'.

Of the original ten, 'Blue Boy' and 'Sailor Boy' came out of the German seeds, the others from England. It was 'Blue Boy' that led the parade (Figure 14). The plant had many good traits; if there were any bad ones, no one noticed. There seemed to be everything to please professional as well as amateur growers—ease of propagation, bounteous numbers of dark blue flowers, and flexible leaf stalks that didn't mind being cramped for shipping. 'Sailor Boy' differed only slightly. Even by today's standards it is a free-flowering plant. The foliage is glossy and green, the blossoms bright sea-blue.

'Admiral' has a noticeable tendency to grow flat. The leaves, a deep dull green, are quilted and cupped downward, ovate with slightly cordate base and an almost smooth margin. The flowers in clusters of three to five, are borne freely above the foliage, and their color is a dark blue, tinged violet.

'Amethyst' (Figure 15) grows more upright, with ovate leaves of medium green, tinged purple on the reverse, and slightly quilted, with dentate edges. The flowers are large, and appear in generous quantities of six to eight well above the foliage. The variety name indicates flower color, and the top petals tend toward a deeper shade.

'Viking' (Figure 16) is another compact plant, with a flat habit of growth. The dark green leaves have a light streak up the center, with undersides of reddish purple. At maturity the leaves have a glossy quilted appearance, and they form a beautiful rosette of rich green color, with petioles flushed maroon. The dark purple flowers are small, but they make large clusters of five to seven on every stalk.

'Mermaid' also grows as a compact plant, with small round leaves of a glossy medium green. The flowers are light blue, and they appear in generous numbers.

'Norseman' (Figure 17) makes a compact rosette, with ovate leaves disposed to incline. The foliage gives a velvety appearance, with attractive quilting. The flowers are nearly true blue, and they appear profusely. So fine is this variety, collectors still treasure it.

'Neptune' is another of the original ten that competes well in any company. It makes a flat plant with obovate leaves that are quilted and shiny, cupping upward and usually spooned. The reddish undersides and petioles contrast with the rich green upper surfaces. The medium-purple flowers come profusely.

'Commodore' grows into a very large plant, with leaves nearly 5 inches long and 3 inches wide, cupped downward, dark green with

FIGURE 14

'Blue Boy'

FIGURE 15

'Amethyst'

FIGURE 16

'Viking'

FIGURE 17

'Norseman'

purple reverses and deeply quilted. The flowers of dark reddish purple grow on short stalks in clusters of six to eight. They do not appear in great quantity, but the plant as a whole is showy, and originally created considerable attention when well grown.

'No. 32' forms a perfect plant with a flat habit of growth, although new foliage is apt to reach upward. The ovate olive-green leaves, slightly dentate and always cupped, have noticeable veining, and beautifully contrasting reddish reverses. The rounded flowers are orchid-violet, just clearing the foliage, and in clusters of six or seven.

Walter Oertel, the man who was foreman of the potted-plant division of Armacost & Royston at the time when these violets were introduced, used this soil mixture for them: 4 parts oak leafmold, 1 part sand, and ½ part steer manure, with the addition of some bonemeal.

After several years of propagating violets, and shipping them wholesale all over the world, Armacost & Royston discontinued this part of their business because the plants were going to growers who did not understand the needs of saintpaulia and consequently found their performance disappointing. When we look back at the lack of cultural information, it seems a miracle that the African-violet survived. Certainly it has great stamina. How fortunate are we today to have at hand complete cultural information about saintpaulias from two national societies which maintain a continuing research program.

INFINITE VARIETY

Even with all the lack of knowledge, collecting saintpaulias was a pleasant, restful undertaking in those early days. Only the species S. *ionantha* was in commerce, and in the 1940's if you had ten different varieties, you had something pretty special. Today growing the various species alone takes considerable space, not to mention the thousands of named varieties.

The first double-flowered African-violet on record was a sport of 'Blue Boy' found in 1939 by a Michigan grower, Edward J. Wangbichler (Figure 18). It was nearly ten years later that more and better doubles were introduced. Since that time there have been remarkable improvements. Now there are doubles in every color classification with all types of foliage and growth habits.

The Fringette series from Fischer Greenhouses were the first African-violets with frilled and ruffled petals, but this is a trait which may be found today in countless varieties. Their leaves may show the same tendency toward waviness along the margins, even intricate crimping and curling.

FIGURE 18

'Double Blue Boy'

'Fantasy' was the first of a new line of African-violets with blossoms rayed, streaked, or splotched with a different color or deeper shade. Then there was 'Lady Geneva', a sport of 'Blue Boy' and the first variety with white-edged dark-colored flowers. Now there are many Genevas, and the edging may be white, pink, chartreuse, or other contrasting color. There are also bicolors.

The number of varieties with star-shaped flowers has increased in recent years. While the usual saintpaulia flower is quite irregular, with two upper lobes and three lower ones, those of star shape have five lobes of almost equal size and equidistant from one another. The first such variety named was 'Star Sapphire', in the early 1950's by the Pennsylvania firm of Robert Craig and Company. In the usual ten-year pattern of progress, by 1962 hybridizers were lavishing their talents on star shapes, and already one leading grower offered twenty-eight different varieties in a rainbow of colors with all foliage types represented.

There are numerous strains and series recognized (Figure 19). A series, such as Caravan, T.V., or Longifolia, usually sets apart a group of varieties with some special characteristic, but all produced by one grower. The series name has more to do with commercial promotion than with botanical distinctions. On the other hand, strains may arise as mutations of existing varieties. For instance, any variety may develop what are Supreme characteristics. Almost any plant may be "spooned," or produce leaves of an exaggerated cupped form, as with 'Spooned Neptune' (Figure 20).

The Supremes are mutations of varieties whose names carry the extra descriptive term, as 'Blue Boy Supreme' (Figure 21). Foliage is usually brittle and heavier, while displaying the same varietal pattern. Flowers are not so freely borne, but they are larger than the variety normally produces. The DuPont strain was characterized by thick, hairy, quilted leaves, somewhat curled and with a piecrust edge (Figure 22). It was slow-growing, not very prolific, but when in bloom produced very large flowers crowded on a few stems. Flowers measured 2½ to 3 inches across. Good & Reese, Inc., of Ohio, produced in 1949 a beautiful numbered series—the DuPont Blue Hybrids. Mrs. William K. DuPont will long be remembered for the contributions that originated in her greenhouses in Wilmington, Delaware. She named only two, both very lovely: 'Christina' and 'Blue Delaware'.

The Amazons, developed by R. A. Brown in Georgia, were very

FIGURE 19

'Bicolor'

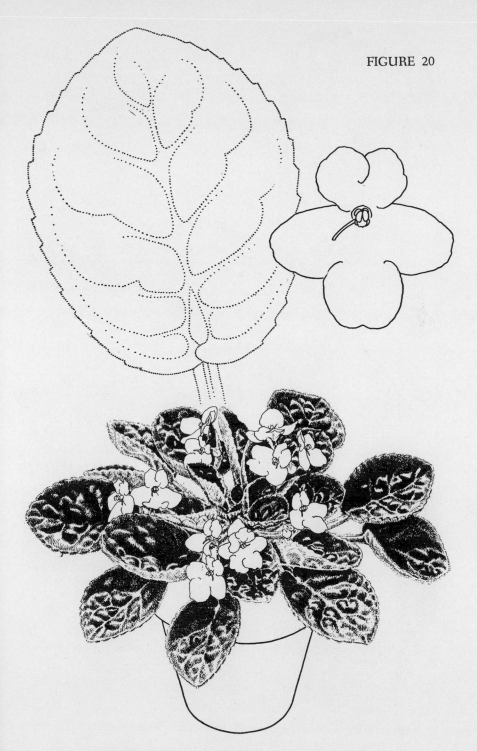

FIGURE 20

'Neptune,' with Spooned Foliage

FIGURE 21

'Blue Boy Supreme'

134

FIGURE 22

'DuPont Lavender Pink'

FIGURE 23

Variegated Type, 'DuPont Lavender Pink'

like DuPonts, but the Browns reported that the leaves inclined "to cut down slightly and in the blue series the leaf edges are dentate."

There are also saintpaulias of miniature size, quite the opposite of the Supremes. The plant spread of a true miniature stays at 6 inches or less at maturity; if the spread reaches 8 inches at maturity, the plant is considered a semi-miniature. Flowers, too, are proportionately smaller, and a small-growing plant with large flowers rates only the term "semi-miniature." Some of these varieties occur as mutants of standard kinds—'Miniature Sailor Girl', for example. Others arise out of breeding programs that are aimed at developing smaller plants. For the collector with insufficient space, miniatures are the answer— the window that once accommodated only twelve standard varieties may afford space for fifty miniatures.

Certain characteristics seem possible for almost any variety. An all-white stalk or a few all-white leaves are not evidence of a true albino. Plants with very light sections often lack vitality and the departure does not survive as fixed. There is usually little stamina or longevity in the pale areas of growth.

Variegation of foliage may appear on any saintpaulia, depending upon cultural conditions, but the characteristic sometimes sticks, as in the varieties which always have an irregular greenish-yellow-to-white area at the leaf base (Figure 23). This is called "girl" foliage, al-though the term has nothing to do with the plant's sex—all saint-paulias bear "perfect" flowers, i.e., flowers with both pistil and stamens (Figure 24).

Occasionally a standard violet (Figure 25) will have a tendency to develop stolons similar to those produced by the related episcias de-scribed in Chapter 15. The drawing of 'Orchid Beauty' (Figure 26) shows the formation of these young plants. Whatever the cause of this, it is only one of the countless traits that make the hobby of African-violets so much fun. Of course, a variety that actually creeps or climbs, with petioles joining the main stem at relatively distant points, probably has S. *grotei* or some other trailing species in its genetic makeup. 'Sky Trailer' is an example of such a variety. It will cascade beautifully off the edge of a shelf or out of a hanging basket.

COLOR AND FORMS

The color of saintpaulias is a not-too-constant quality. In fact, it seems to me after we decide saintpaulias have a range from deep, intense purple through blue-violet, wine-red, and pink-violet to rose,

FIGURE 24

'Blue Girl'

FIGURE 25

'Orchid Beauty'

FIGURE 26

'Orchid Beauty,' Hanging-Basket Type

FIGURE 27

'Pink Beauty'

FIGURE 28

'Ruffles'

FIGURE 29

'White Lady'

Star Girl

Clementine

Sugar
Babe

Ruffled Queen

Pansy

Flower forms of African Violets, showing some

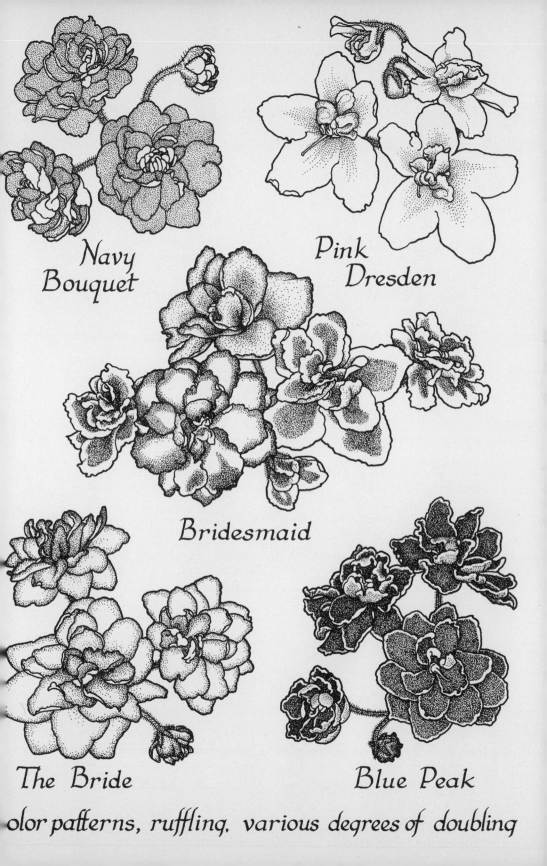

Navy
Bouquet

Pink
Dresden

Bridesmaid

The Bride

Blue Peak

olor patterns, ruffling, various degrees of doubling

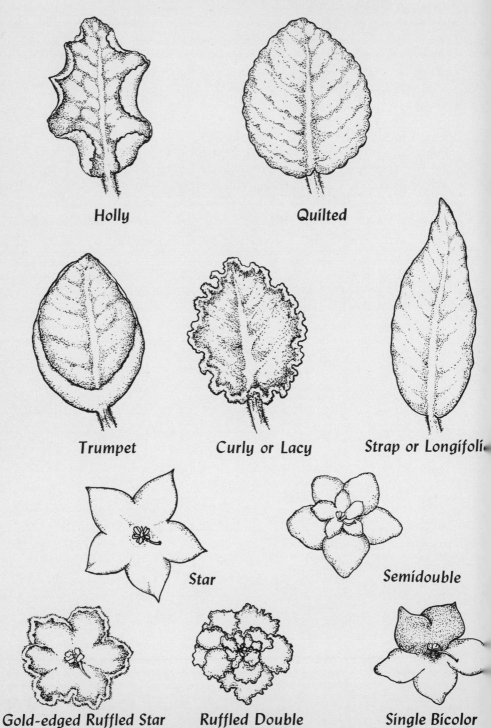

FIGURE 32

ADDITIONAL LEAF AND BLOSSOM TYPES

Holly

Quilted

Trumpet

Curly or Lacy

Strap or Longifoli

Star

Semidouble

K. BOURKE

Gold-edged Ruffled Star

Ruffled Double

Single Bicolor

THE OLD FAVORITES   147

pink, blush, and white, that we have about told the color story. To
give each variety a symbol and place it exactly on a finely graded color
chart is hardly possible or worthwhile. I have tried this method with
several charts and at different seasons. It was a frustrating business.
The saintpaulia that today is Red Violet 4, may after a week of cloudy
weather be nearer Red Violet 6. The variety that in one soil is blue,
under more alkaline conditions may be orchid. We can never be
arbitrary about saintpaulia color.

These early favorites are rarely grown anymore and not to be found
in most growers' lists where even the handsome newer hybrids are
superseded year after year. However, these old ones are still appreci-
ated by many of us who "came to violets" about the same time
some of those did. It is interesting that flower shows today sometimes
have classes for "The Oldies."

11

PROFITS FROM YOUR PLANTS

Money was made, not to command our will,
But all our lawful pleasures to fulfill.
Cowley

Some of our best growers today were hobbyists yesterday. They saw opportunity all around them, especially in the increasing demand for the less common varieties of doubles, the crinkled-leaved and ruffled-leaved types, the various bicolors, variegateds, and stars, and the plants with flowers of unusual shadings or different habits of growth. A few years ago commercial houses catered to the demands of florists rather than to those of collectors. Today they serve both and carry tremendous stocks, sometimes offering several hundred varieties. Even so, "the little fellow" still has a good chance, for local hobbyists and collectors—and travelers too—like to see what they are buying and enjoy an opportunity for personal selection.

After you decide to sell African-violets, there will be many consultations and decisions before the first sale. Some residential areas are zoned for business and others are not; check with your local government. Even if you live in a restricted area, mail-order may be a possible outlet for your plants. In any event, consult with your insurance representative, the Commissioner of Taxes, and the Department of Agriculture at your state capital. Some states require that greenhouse, or fluorescent-grown, ornamentals be inspected periodically;

148

others do not. Get the facts on this from your state before you begin to sell plants.

As a supplier of saintpaulias, you may sell unrooted leaves, rooted leaves, small potted plants (in or out of bloom), specimens in bloom, seeds or seedlings. Any of these may be marketed retail or wholesale, locally or by mail. You can get a good idea of current prices by studying growers' catalogues. Obviously some varieties can command better prices than others.

To begin local selling, advertise in your newspaper. Be willing to go before local garden clubs with a demonstration-lecture about some phase of saintpaulia culture. Invite nearby societies and other clubs to come to an open house; for this day you might establish a rule of no sales but give a small plant to each visitor—this will create good will and a continuing return of new business. To sell by mail, advertise in regional and national gardening magazines. If you have something really special, make it known through advertisements in the African-violet magazines. For example, you might specialize and use a motto, such as "The House of Miniatures" or "Collectors of the Best Pinks."

Your African-violet business will be successful if you sell plants in perfect health and correctly labeled. These conditions are primary. If you meet them, other problems will arise less frequently and will be easier to solve.

SOME SUCCESS STORIES

An acquaintance in Minnesota specializes in saintpaulia seeds. By keeping informed on new findings in the field of genetics, she is able to harvest high-quality seeds year after year. At first these were sold by mail in lots of 100 for one dollar. Special crosses sometimes netted twice that amount. Finally the good reputation of her hybrid seeds brought the inquiry of a leading firm. Would she be interested in selling her seeds exclusively to them for resale? Realizing the savings in paper work, and the advantage of steady income from growing seeds on a contract basis, she agreed. Now these relatively few seed-producing plants support all of her gardening activities, including the operation of a small home greenhouse. More recently she has begun to sell leaf cuttings and small plants to local customers—not many, but enough to increase the profit and pleasure.

I've known a number of amateur growers who eventually went into business. First they filled their windows with African-violets, then installed fluorescent lights to provide more and more indoor growing space—a series of tables with lights above, then double- or triple-decked benches arranged efficiently to utilize as much floor space as possible within a basement, attic, or other room. When these areas are kept clean, and they usually are, they are pleasant to visit, and I am sure that while the owners realize a profit, they must enjoy caring for the plants, too.

One well-known grower in Connecticut started a booming business by cross-pollinating a few hybrid gloxinias that grew on his sunporch. Future generations of these seedlings brought so much success that he found it necessary to build a small greenhouse, then another, another, and still another. Now there are six greenhouses, the last four being full commercial sizes ranging from 2500 square feet up to twice that space. When this grower decided to go into the plant business on a full-time basis, he wisely added a line of the best named African-violets, plus a lengthy list of related plants, other gesneriads, which make perfect companions in the commercial greenhouse as well as in window gardens.

I have a friend who started a plant business, with considerable emphasis on African-violets, after her children went to college. Until that time, she had only a casual interest in her outdoor garden, and the usual house collection of wax begonias, geraniums, and grape ivies. Then she began to study the fascinating worlds of begonias and saintpaulias. First came membership in two local groups, one a branch of the American Begonia Society, the other an African-violet club. Soon she built a small greenhouse attached to the dining room and had plants growing upstairs and under lights. Blue ribbons festooned the bulletin board above her potting bench, and within ten years this enjoyable hobby turned into a thriving business that now promises to provide a more than ample retirement income.

Surely there is a lesson to learn from these success stories—all of which are true. Each of these people started with just a few African-violets. Soon there were many more. Successful as amateur growers, they only gradually became professional with a hobby turning into a thriving business. While the idea of making money from such a pleasant occupation as growing saintpaulias is tempting, an apprenticeship of sound growing experience is essential—a period of learning to walk before there is any question of starting to run.

12

HOW TO START A CLUB

Half the fun of growing saintpaulias is knowing the other people who share your enthusiasm. And there are lots of them. Perhaps right in your town you have noticed ten or twelve houses with African-violets in the windows. Certainly you have a neighbor who grows them. No plant so easily started from a leaf ever stays in one house. In fact, in a small community where people know each other, you can almost see the pretty epidemic spread, as plants from gift leaves come to flowering size in one window after another.

If there is no club of saintpaulia fanciers in your town, why don't *you* start one? Everything worthwhile starts with some one person's enthusiastic efforts. Before 1946 there wasn't a national society either, but there were plenty of fascinated people wanting to know more about their favorite houseplant, and they turned out to be real joiners too. Today the African-violet societies are among the largest horticultural organizations in the world, and they hold national conventions and shows annually all over this country. There are also many African-violet clubs in foreign lands and, if you travel, it's fun to attend a meeting, as I have done in London.

HOW TO FORM A CLUB

So many local clubs have now been formed that there's a wealth of experience at hand to guide you with yours. Why not start by making a list of possible members? Invite them to your house for coffee some afternoon, or if you know that a number of men are interested, make it an evening meeting with a friendly hour or so complete with re-

151

freshments. Write about your plans to one of the societies. (Addresses are given under Information at the end of this book.) Ask for a brochure on membership with application blanks for the approximate number you expect.

Set the time and place—your home, that of a friend with a particularly good saintpaulia collection, or if it looks like a crowd, a club room. Do some invitation telephoning but follow up with a card as a reminder of place, date, hour, and purpose of meeting. It's nice to have people show up on the right day!

FIRST MEETING

Keep it informal. You are planning a friendly club with a friendly purpose. No use getting excited about *Robert's Rules of Order*—at this point, anyway. Get someone to help with introductions, if prospective members aren't likely to know each other. Have a greeter at the door who can break the ice before it forms, and maybe name cards to pin on, a practice I favor highly, being poor on names myself!

From those present, select temporary officers—president, vice-president, secretary, and treasurer to serve until permanent officers can be elected. Invite someone who can talk about the benefits to be derived from joining forces, and about the opportunities for fun and knowledge in one of the national societies. Possibly an already affiliated neighboring club will send one of its officers to help answer questions that arise in every first meeting.

It will be a good idea to appoint some committees right off, especially the one to draw up a constitution and by-laws. The chairman of this committee can get a sample copy of the constitution of one of the national societies to serve as guide. Your group probably won't want to make any changes for a while. You can always amend later.

Try to decide on the next meeting time, and also maybe the place of the next meeting, *before* refreshments. You can never get to it once your guests start exchanging experiences and begin asking, "How do *you* make them bloom?"

SECOND MEETING

Real organization comes out of the second meeting, but I think there should also be a program following the business. Perhaps you can arrange a question-answer Stump-the-Experts party. There are always some who know a lot, and some who are interested but know nothing. If you sense timidity and a backwardness about coming forward with some really "dumb" queries, have people write their questions on slips of paper. Collect these in a hat and let the experts take turns drawing and answering—if they can.

A local florist or grower might be a good speaker for Meeting Number Two. Perhaps your local garden club will have an experienced saintpaulia fan to lend you for the evening. Maybe this is the occasion for a Plant or Leaf Exchange. Later you might have a Clinic. Let members bring their ailing plants for advice. However, be sure to warn everyone about the danger of contaminating healthy African-violets at home if they place among them the invalid just back from Clinic. That plant needs two months of isolation before entering into family life again. A plant can leave home suffering only a lack of humidity but return with a touch of mite!

Here is a list of essential business for the chairman to try to get through at this second meeting:

1. Choose a name.

2. Decide on a regular time and place of meetings. If not possible, at least settle on time and place of *next* meeting.

3. Adopt a constitution and by-laws, if that committee is ready to make a report.

4. Appoint a nominating committee of three.

5. Appoint other committees: *Membership*—Those who attended the first meeting should be put down as Charter Members, if they turn out to be joiners. Plans should be made to invite all others of the community who might be interested. *Reception*—A host- and hostess-group to make newcomers feel welcome. *Program*—Most important, for by this committee interest waxes or wanes, and the new club lives or dies. This group is responsible for securing speakers, transporting them, and making them welcome. (*It should also plainly tell each one how much time is allowed for speaking.* Watch out for speakers who just run on and on.) *Publicity*—Works right along with Program Committee. *Refreshment*—Do plan to feed more than the mind. *Ways and Means*—Right off your club will incur expenses, usually more than membership dues will cover. Later you may need other committees for Door Prizes (unless Ways and Means takes charge of this), Telephoning, "Good Cheer" (to keep in touch with members who are ill), Year Book, and Library. Don't get too complex till your club gets healthily started with saintpaulias as the main theme.

6. Introduce speaker.

7. Thank the speaker orally (have secretary send a note of appreciation afterwards), and adjourn the meeting for social purposes. If you

have a door prize—maybe someone has too many African-violets; that *can* happen—have the drawing for it and the presentation before the formal adjournment for refreshment.

SOME GOOD PROGRAMS

Programs full of vitality and useful information will keep members coming to every meeting, and clubs with frequent perfect attendance are the ones that really get things done. There are certain basic topics that you will want to cover at least once a year. These will probably include general culture, propagation, pest control, and grooming plants for show.

Plan a program on growing plants the fluorescent way. You could get a speaker from the Indoor Light Society for this. If possible, have this meeting in the home of a member who is already successful with African-violets cultivated under artificial light. In the spring, perhaps right after showtime, members will appreciate a good speaker, or panel discussion, on caring for African-violets through the summer. And a demonstration on hybridizing and seed growing always draws enthusiastic response. Again, this is a topic that lends itself to discussion at the home of a member who grows seedlings. An arrangers' workshop with saintpaulia cut flowers the star performers makes an outstanding program. A slide show of African-violet relatives, the other gesneriads, will give members a knowledge of plants that require similar culture. You could get a speaker from one of the sister organizations, of gloxinias, for instance.

Schedule an annual tour in late winter or spring to see the outstanding collections of three or four members. If your society is in easy distance of a commercial grower, make arrangements to see his plants. Unless your group is quite small, let him know in advance so that your visit can be made at a convenient time. Whenever you tour saintpaulia collections, try to abide by these general visiting rules:

1. Let pets and small children enjoy the day at home or with a sitter; otherwise you will be put in the hectic position of trying to keep them out of the plants, and this will stifle your own enjoyment of the tour and probably annoy your host.

2. Don't smoke unless your host invites you to.

3. Stay on the walkways provided. Bulky clothing and large handbags can do much damage to plants along the aisles; be careful.

4. Don't handle plants. If you would like to make closer inspection

of a variety, request the grower to show it to you. Ask for permission before you take pictures.

5. Don't wear out your welcome; chances are your club would enjoy coming back. After the grower gives valuable time to escort your group through the greenhouse, it is only fair to purchase something as a return.

The libraries of the societies provide a wealth of material for outstanding programs. Besides numerous sets of 35mm. color slides, there are Program Packets on many interesting subjects. Current information about the library is given in each issue of the society magazines.

YOUR CLUB'S PROSPERITY

Most club activities require funds in the treasury. Every member who pays dues promptly adds to a club's strength, but first-rate shows and good programs call for the development of a really sturdy Department of Finance. While the Ways and Means Committee bears this responsibility, they will want to enlist the experience and cooperation of all—and there are a number of ways for a club to earn money and at the same time learn more about saintpaulias.

HAVE A PLANT SALE. This is the most obvious way to swell a treasury. Young plants in bloom, labeled and well-groomed, sell readily, both at your own club meetings and at special sales. For example, you might begin months ahead of holiday time to ready plants for a weekend sale staged at a local supermarket or with some other firm willing to cooperate. Most members can contribute one or more plants, and it's a good idea for the best growers to take turns at being on hand to answer questions.

There are things to avoid about plant-selling if your club wants to keep a good reputation. Try not to compete unfairly with local commercial growers. Charge reasonable prices, and in the main sell only saintpaulias and other gesneriads. Be fanatic about this rule: Only plants labeled correctly and free of disease are eligible for the plant sale. If the name of a plant is in doubt, offer it unnamed.

SELL FRESH-CUT LEAVES. This is a practical way of adding funds to your club's treasury. Correctly labeled leaves of standard varieties could command 25 to 50 cents; new or unusual types may bring more, perhaps 75 cents or a dollar each. If these are sold to members, printed instructions probably won't be necessary, but if you offer them at a plant sale to which the public is invited, provide mimeographed instructions in detail, perhaps with some simple sketches drawn by an artistic and knowledgeable grower-member. The easy way to label a leaf is to write the name on a piece of adhesive tape and fasten it to the surface of a leaf.

SELL SUPPLIES IN SMALL QUANTITIES. Members who have only a few plants appreciate this service. A young club in South Dakota found it impossible to buy small quantities of vermiculite and perlite locally, so the Ways and Means Committee bought large economy-sized bags of each, and packaged the mediums in plastic bags, three coffee canfuls to each. These were sold at 25¢ each, thus netting the club a nice profit, but serving members at the same time.

A large African-violet society in Massachusetts buys plastic pots in wholesale lots, and resells them to members. This group also has its own standard growing medium. This is available at 35¢ for three pounds, or nine for a dollar. Other items available in small quantities include vermiculite, perlite, labels, and fertilizers. They sell miniature plastic greenhouses also.

Before your club decides to sell supplies, be certain that you will not be taking away bread-and-butter items from a local grower.

RAFFLE OFF A DOOR PRIZE. Most members like this game of chance and are willing to pay nickels or dimes for tickets. How much you charge is dependent, of course, on the value of the door prize. A well-grown standard African-violet in full bloom, or a started cutting of the newest variety on the market will add excitement to this aspect of club activity. Members contribute the door-prize plants. Avoid having to beg local commercial growers or mail-order suppliers for door prizes. If they offer them, fine, but otherwise, no.

STAGE A PLANT AUCTION. For real fun, nothing equals this method of gaining funds for a club. Members contribute the plants (healthy and correctly labeled), and bidding may start at any appropriate level, depending on age of plant, cultural excellence, and variety.

HAVE A WHITE-ELEPHANT SALE. Here's another gala way to make money for your club. Keep to the theme of African-violets, and ask that each package (gift wrapped, perhaps in violet-patterned paper) contain some piece of equipment or item of supply that will help grow better plants. Popular items include pots, a rooting medium, fertilizer, or pieces of small flowering-arranging equipment for use with minia-tures. Select a member with bubbling personality and a keen sense of humor to be your auctioneer.

SELL GARDENING BOOKS. Each year this country's publishers offer many outstanding books about gardening. Except for persons who have access to large bookstores and libraries, fine volumes are often overlooked. Your club can do a real service by having a member get on the publishers' mailing list, to receive announcements of new titles. Review these frequently, and take orders when possible. Most publishers grant a forty percent discount on even a small quantity of books handled this way, so your club can realize profit on every copy sold. In addition, I think it's a good idea to own and to keep on hand two or three copies of a good book on African-violet culture that can be on display at each meeting.

13

HOW TO GIVE A SHOW
AND JUDGE IT

No rule is so general,
Which admits not some exception.
Robert Burton

Of course "there's no business like show business," and I don't mean just in the theater. Nothing benefits a new club more than putting on an African-violet show, for almost everyone who attends wants to grow saintpaulias too. Membership rises, enthusiasm within the old membership is stimulated, and everybody starts growing better plants because everybody has found out more about them.

YOUR FIRST SHOW

If your club is almost a year old, it's time to put on the first show. And that takes planning, some six months of it for an ambitious project, and six to nine months must really be allowed for the development of fine show plants. A show requires somebody at the top with the disposition of a saint, the judgment of a Solomon, and a very cool head indeed. Many last-minute crises develop when plants are the main performers, because even with careful planning there is only so much that can be done ahead of show day.

Furthermore, everyone can't win a blue ribbon. We all have favorite plants, and it's hard sometimes to avoid hurt feelings when they don't look as good to the judges as to us. However, be a good

158

sport. Maybe yours will get the honors next time. Meanwhile why not quietly examine the blue-ribbon winner? Why not try to find out how it surpasses your entry? Sometimes judges make critical comments on non-winning plants. Such a practice can be very helpful, provided the judges are tactful and kindly in criticism (they try to be), and you are able to accept an impersonal criticism impersonally. An adverse judgment indicates flaws in the plant, you understand; it is not aimed at you!

Don't attempt too much at your first show, particularly if none of the membership has had much to do with flower shows before. There is still no substitute for experience. Your first show might be only a well-displayed exhibit of clearly-labeled varieties—no blue ribbons or awards given. It would still be most interesting to the average public, many of whom don't even know there are other than plain blue, purple, or pink African-violets. It's better to do well what you attempt and have everybody feel good about it than to try to put on an elaborate show with many classes only to discover a host of problems that you just haven't had the experience to solve.

One service your first show can render is the answering of questions. Let the best growers among you take turns at the Question Booth, where people can get the information they long for on "how to make them bloom." Those who try to answer this, of course, need plenty of stamina!

Eventually, you will want, beside the usual classifications by color, educational exhibits that show how to propagate from leaves, how to cross-pollinate, how to grow from seed, various methods of growing plants in water, how to pot—and most useful of all—a clinic on pests and diseases, their symptoms, prevention, and cure.

Your clinic might include these departments: Pharmacy (suggestions on using dusting sulfur, Fermate, V-C 13); Surgery (how to remove sucker growth, cut off rotted sections of crown or roots, cut apart a heavily crowned plant); Potting; Watering; Ways to Increase Humidity; even How to Make Your African-Violets Bloom, with exhibits of methods and plant foods.

Then you may want some artistic displays of plants in bubble bowls, aquariums, or terrariums; colorful groupings for dining or coffee tables; groups with other plants in tray or dish gardens; plants growing in high-stemmed goblets; arrangements of plants on tiered tables, step plant-stands, or on Lazy Susans, and also arrangements of fresh-cut flowers with or without accessories. (Year Book Classes can certainly be matters for future consideration.)

SHOW COMMITTEES

Get your first show off to a good start by including the entire membership in the preliminary plans. As a group, you will need to vote on having a show at a time that will be convenient for the majority. The president of your club can appoint the Show Chairman, and also chairmen for the following committees: (1) Schedule, (2) Staging, (3) Properties, (4) Entries, (5) Classifications, (6) Publicity, (7) Judges, (8) Hospitality, and (9) Clean-up. In addition, some groups have found it helpful to have committees in charge of awards, special exhibits, tickets (if admission is charged), and watering. For a small show, you could easily combine some of these committees.

What follows here are fairly general suggestions based on the *Judges & Exhibitors African Violet Handbook,* prepared for the African Violet Society of America (AVSA) by Ruth G. Carey (available from her, 3900 Garden Drive, Knoxville, Tenn. 37918, for $1.50), and the *Guide for Judges and Exhibitors,* edited for Saintpaulia International (SI) by Lucile Rainsberger, available from Saintpaulia International, P. O. Box 10604, Knoxville, Tenn. 37919.

The Show Chairman is in full charge of the show but consults with all the other chairmen. It is a good idea for this group to determine the *exact* date of the show, even though the club may vote on a general time. Now let's consider the work of each committee.

1. *Schedule Committee* takes care of having a schedule printed and presenting copies to the membership well in advance of the show. This includes all decisions made by the show committees, such as time and place of show, when entries will be received and the time entries close, hour show opens, time for judging to begin, time exhibitors may remove exhibits, and length of time plants must be in exhibitor's possession (usually three months).

One of this committee's first considerations is the amount of space that will be available for exhibits. With this information firmly in mind, classes are set up. To do this well, consider the horticultural and artistic abilities of all members. For example, the plants of one grower may so far exceed all others in size and floriferousness that they will need a special class or be considered as an exhibit that is not to be judged at all.

Some schedules list specific varieties that might be exhibited under each color classification. Others, such as the sample schedule included here, list only colors. You will need to state also whether an exhibitor can make only one or more entries in each class.

A Sample Schedule for an Amateur Division

SECTION I—Single-blossom standard-type plants

Class 1 Pinks
          2 Whites
          3 Orchids and lavenders
          4 Dark blues and purples
          5 Medium and light blues
          6 Reds and wines
          7 Bicolors, multicolors, Genevas, and variegated blossoms

SECTION II—Double-blossom standard-type plants

Class 8 Pinks
          9 Whites
       10 Orchids and lavenders
       11 Dark blues and purples
       12 Medium and light blues
       13 Reds and wines
       14 Bicolors, multicolors, Genevas, and variegated blossoms

SECTION III—Single-blossom Supreme-type plants

Class 15 Pinks
       16 Whites
       17 Orchids and reds
       18 Blues and purples
       19 Bicolors, multicolors, Genevas, and variegated blossoms

SECTION IV—Double-blossom Supreme-type plants

Class 20 Pinks
       21 Whites
       22 Orchids and reds
       23 Blues and purples
       24 Bicolors, multicolors, Genevas and variegated blossoms

SECTION V—Standard and Supreme plants with variegated foliage, single or double blossoms

Class 25 Pinks
       26 Whites

27 Orchids and lavenders
28 Dark blues and purples
29 Medium and light blues
30 Reds and wines
31 Bicolors, multicolors, Genevas, and variegated blossoms

SECTION VI—Miniature and semi-miniature plants, green or variegated foliage, single or double blossoms

Class 32 Pinks
33 Whites
34 Orchids and lavenders
35 Dark blues and purples
36 Medium and light blues
37 Reds and wines
38 Bicolors, multicolors, Genevas, and variegated blossoms

SECTION VII—Mutants, sports, and seedlings never before entered in a convention show

Class 39 Mutants and sports
40 Seedlings

SECTION VIII—Species and trailers

Class 41 Hybrid trailers
42 Saintpaulia species

SECTION IX—Terrariums: All live plants, African-violets predominating and in bloom

Class 43 Terrariums

SECTION X—Artistic Arrangements

Class 44 "Indian Summer"—Saintpaulia blossoms with fruit and/or grain and fall-colored foliage.
45 "Christmas at Home"—Saintpaulia with pine or cedar branches; spray snow may be used.
46 "Study in Geometrics"—Line arrangement using cut African-violet blossoms, other flowers and foliage permitted.
47 "Sunshine and Snow"—An arrangement of white cut African-violet blossoms in white container, on a yellow fabric. Ferns, foliage, and other flowers permitted.
48 "From the Land of Lilliput"—Arrangement of cut African-violet blossoms from any miniature variety; other foliage permitted. African-violets must predominate.

SECTION XI—Artistic Plantings

Class 49 "Woodland Fantasy"—A saintpaulia planting with wood fern and/or other roadside material.

50 "Gateway to the North"—A planting of foliage and African-violets.

51 "Wildwood"—A planting in driftwood or other weathered wood.

52 "Klompen Dancers"—A planting in a wooden shoe.

53 "Invitation to the Woods"—African-violet plant or plants in a naturalistic setting. Rocks, shells, ferns, other material permitted.

54 "Birds of Our State"—African-violet plant or plants used with ceramic birds in suitable setting. Other plant material permitted.

55 "Family Album"—Composition of African-violet plant or plants with other gesneriads.

JUDGING AND SCORING

Your schedule should state the method of judging the club wishes to use, either competitive or merit. The competitive form of judging is preferable. It tends to elevate the standard of your show if only one blue, one red, and one white award is given in each class or section, if your schedule is classified according to varieties. By the merit method of judging, several blue ribbons may be awarded in each class of section. At first this seems a nice gesture, but it certainly takes away from the honor of receiving a blue ribbon. In a large show honorable mentions may be given if entries are worthy. Award a Tricolor or Best-of-the-Show to the most outstanding specimen plant among blue-ribbon winners, but only a plant that rates 95 or more points should qualify for this distinction.

It is most helpful if the schedule includes the scales of points that will be used in judging. The publication of these allows exhibitors and judges to work from the same standard and secures greater uniformity in judging. Here are some of the point scales used by the national societies—AVS and SI. These are given here for your *general* guidance; they may be somewhat changed for your own purposes in the course of time.

	Scale of Points	
	AVS	SI
1. Specimen plants		
Leaf pattern or form (Symmetry of plant)	30	25
Floriferousness (quantity of bloom according to variety)	25	30
Condition (cultural perfection; freedom from disease, insects and marred foliage)	20	25
Size of bloom (according to variety)	15	15
Color of bloom (according to variety)	10	5
	100	100
2. Seedlings		
Leaf pattern or growth habit	20	35
Floriferousness	25	20
Condition	10	
Size of bloom (medium to large)	15	10
Color of blossoms	10	
Distinction (improvement or difference from any named variety	20	20
Strength of bloom stalk		15
	100	100

3. Miniatures

   Miniatures and semi-miniatures may be judged by the
   same scale of points as standard varieties, except in
   number of blooms, which should be according to
   variety.

   A mature miniature will have a leaf span of 6 inches or
   under with flowers and leaves proportionately smaller
   than those of a standard variety. A semi-miniature
   will not exceed an 8-inch diameter for a mature plant.
   Leaves may be larger than on the miniature. Bloom is
   comparable in size to that of standard varieties.

4. Arrangements

	Scale of Points	
	AVS	SI
Design	35	30
Color combination	20	25
Distinction and originality	15	20
Relation to container	10	
Condition	10	10
Suitability of combination of all material	10	15
	100	100

Year Books can also be judged, but are not likely to be included in your club's first show.

5. Points necessary to win ribbons

Blue ribbon	90–100	90–100
Red ribbon	80– 89	80– 89
White Ribbon	70– 79	70– 79
Honorable mention	65– 69	
Best in class	95 or above	95 or above

6. Plantings—Naturalistic or woodland scenes, terrariums, dish gardens, etc.

	Scale of Points	
	AVS	SI
Design and arrangement of planting	40	30
Suitability of materials	25	15
Condition	15	10
Color combination	10	25
Distinction and originality	10	20
	100	100

Give a Sweepstakes Award to the member who wins the most blue ribbons in a show. In case of a tie, include a count of points as follows: Blue ribbon, 3 points; red ribbon, 2 points; white ribbon, 1 point.

2. *Staging Committee* finds a suitable location for the show. The staging chairman must be available prior to the day of the show and until the doors are open to the public. This chairman makes all decisions concerning disposition of space and works out the amount of space to be allotted to each class, while keeping aisles wide enough for entries to be roped off.

The committee should have the following items available: hammer, thumbtacks, wire, screw driver, lettering pens, extra schedules, nails, cloths and rags, string, pins, cardboard and poster board, paint, Scotch tape, tags and stickers, pencils, scissors, measuring tape, brooms, etc.!

In staging some special or individual exhibits or entries, the exhibitor may provide his own metal stand or card table, or luncheon or breakfast table.

Tables with boxes upon them of uniform size used in tiers can be covered with paper or some soft material in a color that blends with all shades of green.

3. *Properties Committee* works with the staging committee and in a small show may be part of it. This group is responsible for the club property that is stored from show to show and for the purchase of entry cards, stickers, ribbons, and so forth.

4. *Entry Committee* has the duty of taking care of every entry in the show, seeing that it is properly named, recorded, and placed. The scheduled classes should be divided among the members so that each is responsible for certain classes.

Each entry should be recorded in a notebook as the exhibitor brings it into the show. Entries in each class should be on a separate page.

A card should be made out for each entry with the exhibitor's name, class, and number in the class on it. This card is placed on the plant with the exhibitor's name folded up and clipped. After judging is completed, the clip is removed so that the exhibitor's name is displayed and the ribbon or award (if any), can be attached by a judges' clerk.

The Entry Committee should see that exhibitors conform to the schedule in placing only one entry in a class, except when a class is divided by color, variety, or other classifications. All entries should be properly labeled as to variety. This committee has the power to disqualify a plant only if it arrives after the deadline for entries is past.

5. *Classification Committee* works with the entry committee and also the schedule committee in helping to list varieties according to color. Two or three members are sufficient. They should be familiar with most varieties and able to recognize them readily. It is important that this committee know which varieties are similar, and the correct names of each variety. They should also be familiar with the evidence of diseases and not hesitate to *disqualify suspicious plants* for the protection of other exhibits. They give advice to the Entry Committee as to the proper classes in which to enter exhibits. If the judges detect what they believe to be an error, they must call it to the attention of the Classification Committee to correct.

6. *Publicity Committee* builds up public interest through posters, radio, and television announcements, and newspaper articles. A detailed account of your show, stressing outstanding exhibits, names of judges and names of all prize winners in all classes should be given to the newspapers after the judging. Newspaper photographers may be invited to attend. A large placard with the scale of points (fully explained as to what each one includes) may be placed where visitors can see how the judges made their decisions.

7. *The Judges Committee* secures judges, sends them schedules,

arranges transportation. The names of judges should be withheld from the public, until after the show. Judges should never enter the exhibition room until the show is completely ready.

Usually three judges suffice for the average show. If a large show is held, two groups of judges may be used, each group judging certain classes.

As to entertaining your judges, that is up to the judging committee. They are usually met at the train, bus, or airport, if they travel in any of these ways. They may be served a light refreshment before judging, then luncheon after judging is completed. The judges' transportation, meals, and hotel (if necessary) should be paid by the club. It is also the duty of the chairman of judges to write a prompt note of thanks to each judge.

The Judges' Clerks serve as attendants to the judges. They should be instructed in their duties and know the rules of the schedule governing the show. Two clerks are recommended for each group of judges, one to record the awards in the entry book, and one to place ribbons or seals on the exhibits. They should be equipped with entry books, ribbons, stickers, pencils, erasers, and extra schedules. Clerks should never volunteer information. They may answer any question, secure needed information, and run errands. They should keep far enough away from the judges to allow them to talk freely. The clerk may also write the judges' comments in the entry book or on a card to be placed with the exhibit if asked to do so by the judges. No one but judges, clerks, and the chairman of judges or general show chairman should be present while the show is being judged.

After judging is completed, the clerks should compile a list of prize-winning exhibits for the club's record and for the publicity chairman.

8. *Hospitality Committee* greets visitors, answers questions, tries to see that plants are not handled; sometimes helps entertain judges.

9. *Cleanup Committee* cleans up the show room after staging is completed (prior to judging). In addition, they see to it that the display area is kept presentable throughout the exhibition, and if necessary, clean the room after the show is closed. Of them, it can be said "they also serve!"

ABOUT JUDGES

Besides being monuments of fairness, courage, and tact, good judges need to have above all a thorough knowledge of varieties; they must recognize the signs of health and illness in order to wisely eliminate any infested or diseased entries; also understand the effects of exposures, fertilization, humidity, and watering. However, if you are putting on a little show with local judges, don't expect such wisdom. Pick people who grow African-violets and let them do the best they can. Shows are supposed to be fun, not exercises in character development. Above all stand by your judges and let it be known that their decisions must be final. If you would rather have an outside judge, write to one of the national societies and ask them for suggestions of qualified judges near your town. (See addresses under Societies at the end of this book.)

Judges can be trained. The societies sponsor schools throughout the country to qualify members as apprentice judges. On occasion, each society puts on a Judging School at the time of the annual convention. At these sessions all aspects of judging are discussed, examinations given, and certificates bestowed on those who are considered qualified.

African-violets, being special plants, require special judging so that the holder of a judge's certificate from the National Council of State Garden Clubs is unlikely to be qualified, unless to her experience with house and garden plants, she also adds knowledge of saintpaulias. If she has this, her experience in judging will be valuable, since the same techniques apply to all horticultural judging. Incidentally, particularly in small clubs, judges should not be disqualified from exhibiting. They should simply bow out to another room while the class in which they are represented is judged by others.

ENTRY CARDS

Here is a typical card for show business.

Section_____

Class_____

Number_____

Entry_____

. . . .

[marked here to fold up]

Name of exhibitor _____

The exhibitor's name is folded over and fastened with a paper clip until judging is finished. Then it may be unfolded and displayed so that congratulations may be personally received and enjoyed by the winners.

SHOW TERMS

Amateur grower. One who grows plants for pleasure, not to sell. Also one who pays *individual* membership dues to a national society.

Commercial grower. One who buys, grows, sells, and advertises plants as a business enterprise, and pays *commercial* membership dues to a national society.

Disqualify. To remove an entry from consideration by the judges because of some defect that is the exhibitor's fault or because it does not conform to schedule. When time permits, the reason for disqualification is written on the entry card.

Eliminate. To remove from consideration by the judges any plant that will have no chance of reward—as a diseased, lopsided, or generally poor specimen.

Entry. Single plant or unit entered in accordance with the schedule's requirements.

Exhibit. Plant or plants on display but not in competition.

Multicolored blossoms. Those of two or more colors.

Sucker. The start of a new plant near the base or in the axil where a petiole joins the main stem.

Two-tone. Flowers with light and dark values of the same color.

Geneva varieties. Having blossoms with white edges.

HINTS ON GROOMING PLANTS FOR SHOWING

Since form and symmetry count for a big 25 or 30 points and can be developed only over a long growing period, start to train your plant in the way it should go the minute it gets into a 2¼-inch pot. Set it firmly in the center and remember the weekly or more frequent quarter turn (always move in one direction, as clockwise) at the window so growth will be even—and characteristic in size, color, and habit. Even plants under fluorescents may need to be turned regularly unless they are placed *directly* beneath the tubes.

If an important leaf in the lowest circle of leaves gets broken off, and there remains a gap like the opening in a six-year-old's teeth, you can train the leaves on each side of the gap to cover it up. Insert small plant labels or toothpicks into the soil at points where they will help to train leaves to fill the space left by the lost leaf, as in Figure 4. Move them each day so as to make the gap narrower. Eventually the urged leaves will take the hint and grow where you have firmly indicated they should. With perfect symmetry established, remove the props.

(If you forget to remove them, and the judges notice, the plant will be disqualified.)

Train to a regular outline. Sometimes one leaf grows out beyond all others. You will have to remove such a one, and then train others to cover up. Irregular plants may be more interesting and perhaps prettier in the window, but show business is different, and in a way, artificial.

Remember that the 25 or 30 points for *floriferousness* are based on quantity of bloom *according to variety*. Blooms, not buds in any stage, are what count. The same holds for *size* of bloom, 15 points. Some varieties are expected to have flowers twice as large as those of others.

Variability in *color,* 10 points, is expected by all good judges who are familiar with the change of color that is wrought in saintpaulias by differences in soil, water, and exposure.

Cultural condition, 20 or 25 points, should be just about perfect, no leaves bleached by sun, no damaged foliage, no suckers, no spots, no insects, no disease traces, no dead bloom stalks. Neither size nor quantity of bloom can help a plant that isn't absolutely at the peak of cultural perfection.

To disbud show plants or not? It takes approximately nine to twelve months for a show specimen to develop from a young plant in a 2¼-inch pot. Some successful exhibitors give the best culture they can to all their plants. Without going to the trouble of disbudding, they select many prize-winning entries a day or two before show time. Many sweepstakes winners disbud doubles ten weeks before show time, singles eight weeks ahead, and Supremes at least twelve weeks. That is Lucile Rainsberger's plan, and whose advice could be better with so many awards to her credit! In fact, she disbuds show plants several months before she allows them to form any buds at all because "it is far easier to space leaves where there is no bloom"; in these early months the plants are forced to put energy into making leaves.

Her fertilizing schedule for show plants is no different from that for all her plants. "The plant that has been grown right doesn't need extra food." Planted in her own version of the Nature's Way formula at the 3-inch-pot stage, they receive at two-week intervals in rotation Atlas Fish Emulsion, Hyponex (7-6-19), and Plant Marvel.

And no "tight shoe" for the Rainsberger specimens. Show plants may be shifted on three times in a year so that there will always be "fresh soil for roots to push into. Small plants go into big pots but these must be watered with care."

Under fluorescents—the preference being for one cool white and one warm white de luxe, when available, otherwise a standard warm white—lights are on twelve to fourteen hours. Lucile says, "When I'm not in a hurry for bloom, twelve hours are enough; when I need a lot of small blooming plants at a specific time, lights are left on fourteen hours. And, about two months before I need flowering plants I put in new tubes. For instance, to push bloom for mid-March, I put in new tubes early in January. New tubes must not be left on as long at first as older tubes. New tubes lose power rather rapidly for about twenty days. Then the loss is little for about a year. I always decrease the light by about two hours for the first month of new-tube use. After that there is no danger of burning foliage."

All mature plants are grown within 3 to 4 inches of tubes (but not new tubes), and they are set no closer in preparation for showing. Plants are moved about at almost every watering time to equalize the light, since it is strongest directly under the center. Strips of white tissue paper, 6 × 8 inches, laid over large leaves prevent bleaching. In general, shelves (not plant tops) and tubes are 12 inches apart for big plants, 10 inches for younger ones.

Lucile urges those developing show entries to keep in mind that each plant is an individual: "not all plants you groom to show are going to make it. Some will flower too soon, some too late. Furthermore, weather can alter schedules." In one hot summer, even with air conditioning in her basement, many of her plants reached show condition a month ahead of time. And records of disbudding, she says, are important because they can be based on your conditions and are the best possible guide to future disbudding.

TEN LITTLE THINGS THAT COUNT A LOT

1. Read the show schedule once more to make sure your plants fit into the classes you have planned them for.

2. Check again to see that all suckers, seed pods, dead or faded flowers, and spent stems have been removed, and that no "neck" is in evidence.

3. Be sure plants show no sign of disease.

4. Have pots spotlessly clean. This adds immeasurably to the spruced-up look of show-bound African-violets. Tuck foil securely over the edge of each pot if foil is used.

5. Label plants as to variety, so that after judging the public knows what it is looking at. (Nothing irritates me—and everyone else—more at a flower show than to see something I really want, and not be able

to find a soul to tell me what it is.) Label also as to ownership. Write your name with pencil, which does not blur as ink does if it gets wet, on a piece of adhesive and fasten it to the bottom of the pot. Then there won't be any question of which plant belongs to you.

6. Get rid of all supports, toothpicks, and the like.

7. Shower plants well near show time to remove dust, but don't let this be a day-before job because a few blooms almost always get knocked off in showering and cleansing. Take care that no residue of spray or water remains. Or if you prefer to brush plants, just go over them again.

8. Water your plants well so they won't get droopy if the exhibition room gets warm.

9. Transport with care—whether six blocks or 600 miles. This is an important part of African-violet show business. (For information on this, read Chapter 14.) And do take grooming aids along; sharp manicure scissors to cut off fading and spent blossoms; a half-inch camel's-hair brush to remove any bit of soil from the leaf stalks and a wider brush for the leaves; and your meat-baster to water the plants at the last minute without the danger of splashing soil particles on a leaf stalk.

10. Lift up blooms so that they are not hidden by foliage, and shift the leaves a little as necessary to make them lie in proper layers.

Since your show plant is a treasure, be sure it gets a thorough spraying right after the show, just in case it has picked up a pest or disease there. Or you might sell your plants—sometimes there is an auction—and let the proceeds go to your research fund. Sometimes it's easier to bring a new plant on to perfection than to help a winner recover from the ordeal of a show.

14

AFRICAN-VIOLETS ARE GOOD TRAVELERS

He that travels much knows much.
Thomas Fuller

Every saintpaulia fancier needs to know how to wrap leaves, and sometimes plants too, for safe mailing or shipping. There will always be specimens at your window that can spare a few leaves to add new varieties to someone else's collection. There will always be occasions when, from your own abundance, you will want to select a plant for a distant friend's birthday or Christmas present. In addition, one of the most important parts of show business is transporting plants so that they arrive in perfect condition. Therefore I am outlining here the methods used by growers to make good travelers of African-violet plants and leaves.

Patents and quarantines may keep you from freely sharing your African-violets with friends around the world or even in this country. Since new saintpaulia cultivars are not often patented, you need to know only that this possibility exists. The quarantine regulations for sending living plant material from state to state and country to country are complex and changeable; at times they may seem insurmountable.

173

PATENTED PLANTS

The purpose of the Plant Patent Law is to insure some monetary return on the investment of time and money that is behind every origination. A plant patent is meant to serve the horticultural scientist in the same way that a patent on an electronics device protects the inventor. The Plant Patent Law of 1930 has not been completely successful. In fact, the steps necessary to patent a new plant are so time-consuming and expensive that it is usually not profitable.

Nevertheless, you may someday encounter a patented African-violet that has a wooden or plastic label stating the plant's name and patent number. Legally you may not propagate this variety vegetatively without permission.

If you are a commercial grower and wish to propagate a patented variety, you may obtain permission by signing a contract with the patent owners. This involves buying the plant labels at a stated fee. You are required to place a label on every plant or leaf you sell, or give away, of a patented variety. For further information write to the United States Patent Office in Washington, D.C.

WRAPPING AND MAILING LEAVES

Importing and exporting plants builds international friendships, and helps us gain new introductions at the same time we share our bounty. This beneficial exchange continues only because the majority follow plant import-export laws. Of necessity these are changeable, and the best procedure is to contact your nearest Plant Quarantine Service of the U. S. Department of Agriculture. Or write to the U. S. Department of Agriculture, Bureau of Entomology and Plant Quarantine, Hoboken, New Jersey.

The inexpensive way to achieve variety is to swap leaves with other collectors or to buy leaves from growers. You can then propagate for yourself and so develop extensive representation. When leaves are exchanged, the aim is to pack them so that they can travel well through the mails to great distances. They should arrive in such fresh condition that full vitality remains to nourish a new crop of plants.

When preparing leaves for mailing, cut the stems longer than usual. This allows the recipient to trim back a stem to fresh tissue before putting it down to root. Wrap the lower third of the stem in moist cotton or tissue, then fold a piece of aluminum foil around the entire stem, crimping the foil together carefully. Place each leaf in a

Trends in Flower Forms. Top left, star type. Right, phlox eye. Center, two doubles with contrasting edgings. Below left, a single with a contrasting edge; right, a striped bicolor. Lyon photos.

Above, Miniature Species and Varieties of Sinningias from Buell, including in the center, S. *pusilla* and lower left, S. *concinna*. Below, left and right, miniature saintpaulias from Lyon: 'Tiny Violet' and 'Baby Pink'. In the center, 'Tom Thumb', a miniature gloxinia from Fischer.

Colorful Gesneriads. Opposite page, upper left, double white African-violet 'Robert O' (Rainsberger hybrid); right, *Kohleria* 'Rongo' (Batcheller hybrid). Middle, left, *Columnea* 'Chipewa', Granger Gardens; center, *Achimenes* 'Red Beauty' and, right, Episcia 'Tricolor', both Lyndon Lyon. Lower left, *Streptocarpus,* Julius Roehrs Co.; right, *Streptocarpus,* Granger Gardens. *Achimenes* photo by Lyon; all other photos Robert Wright, Sr. for *Gesneriad Saintpaulia News.*

The Charm of the Miniatures, as Alma Wright grows and displays them. Above left, *Sinningia* 'Wood Nymph'; right, *X Gloxinera* 'Cupid's Doll'. Below, left, *Sinningia pusilla*; right, *X Gloxinera* 'Ramadeva'. Robert Wright, Jr. photos for *Gesneriad Saintpaulia News.*

small plastic or cellophane bag; or make a suitable envelope of waxed paper, held together with staples or Scotch tape, as in Figure 34.

Place packaged leaves on a cushion of excelsior or shredded newspaper in a cardboard box or mailing tube. Then fill in carefully with more excelsior or newspaper. Finally wrap, tie, and label for parcel post, first class, or air mail. First class and air mail are more expensive, of course, but also quicker and in this transaction speed is of the essence. When considerable distance is involved, valuable leaves may be sent air mail special delivery. The trick is to keep the leaves as short a time as possible out of a growing medium of water or soil, and in transit to maintain moist stems and dry tops. It is also important to prevent any shifting of the leaf during the journey. Wrapping must be thick enough to protect leaves from being crushed in handling, particularly when the box is stamped. In warm weather, punch holes in the heavier coverings to provide some ventilation.

HOW TO WRAP AND SHIP A PLANT

A simple method of wrapping is illustrated in Figures 33 and 34. Materials include: two pieces of waxed paper, one cut in a square and the other a sheet 2 feet long; brown wrapping paper at least 16 inches wide, or newspaper; two widths of brown-gummed, masking, or Scotch tape; a strong corrugated box of appropriate size; and crumpled or shredded newspaper.

Ship plants in soil that is nicely moist, neither dripping wet nor dry. Clay pots are too heavy. Use a plastic pot, or remove the plant from the pot, surround the soil with barely-moist sphagnum moss, and then cover with aluminum foil. Young plants with a leaf spread of 4 to 8 inches usually ship better than smaller or larger ones.

Set the plant on the smaller piece of waxed paper. Then gently but firmly tuck the paper in over the edge of the pot, or around the top of the foil. This serves to hold in the soil and to support the leaves in an almost upright position.

Next lay the plant on its side at the narrow end of the longer piece of waxed paper. With one hand ease the leaves into a straight position; with the other roll at the girth of the pot or foil-covered soil ball until 4 or 5 inches of paper remains. Then fold up the lower end; roll the remainder if length of leaves permits and seal with tape just above the pot rim or foil. The resulting package should have no flare but be perfectly straight.

Plant is set in center of a
square of waxed paper
which is then tucked in
securely over pot rim, to hold
in soil and to support leaves.

Potted plant is then
laid on side and centered
at one end of a 2-foot strip of waxed paper; the
leaves are gently drawn up straight with one hand
as the other rolls paper and pot. Excess paper
at pot end is folded up before last turn, fastened
with 1-inch gummed paper tape.

How to Wrap a Plant or Leaves for Mailing

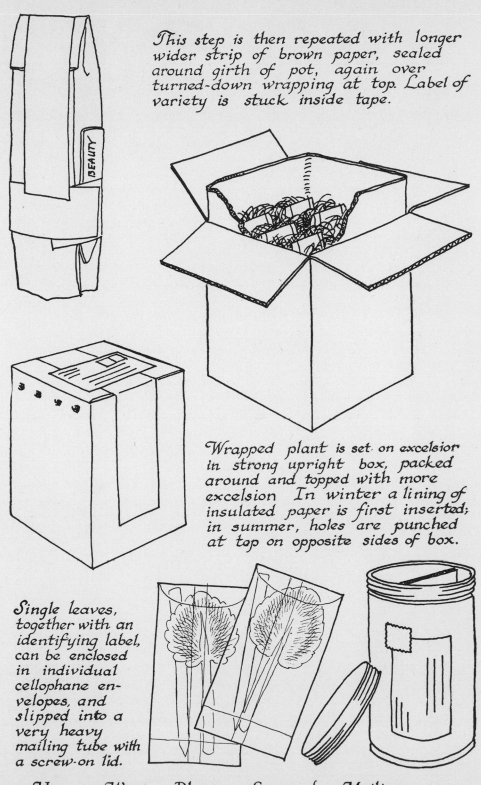

This step is then repeated with longer wider strip of brown paper, sealed around girth of pot, again over turned-down wrapping at top. Label of variety is stuck inside tape.

Wrapped plant is set on excelsior in strong upright box, packed around and topped with more excelsion. In winter a lining of insulated paper is first inserted; in summer, holes are punched at top on opposite sides of box.

Single leaves, together with an identifying label, can be enclosed in individual cellophane envelopes, and slipped into a very heavy mailing tube with a screw-on lid.

How to Wrap a Plant or Leaves for Mailing

The second step of wrapping is then repeated, using the heavy wrapping paper, or about three sheets of newspaper. In cold weather, place the plant on the paper so that enough will remain at top and bottom to fold up. During warm weather, fold up paper at the bottom, but leave the top open so the plant can get more air. The label bearing the name of the variety is tucked into the tape that secures this heavier wrapping.

Finally the plant is placed on crumpled newspaper in a box of heavy corrugated board. It is packed by itself, or in an appropriately larger box, which may hold several plants. Once a plant is packed gently but firmly in the crumpled newspaper—up to the very top—there is no possibility of shifting inside the box.

In winter, wrap a layer of insulated paper, the kind used in bags for frozen food, around the plant after the stuffing has been completed. Finally seal the box at the top and label there. In warm weather, no insulating paper is used, but for aeration punch a line of holes along opposite sides of the package. For summer mailing particularly, excelsior provides better aeration as a packing material, but newspaper of course is more readily available.

African-violets thus carefully packed and labeled will travel well by mail, air, or railway express.

BY CAR TO THE SHOW

Safe transporting of show plants from home to exhibit hall is an important step in winning blue ribbons. And the trip across town can be as hazardous as a cross-country journey. A sudden stop in your own driveway, for that matter, can ruin a fine symmetrical specimen, but it is possible to pack African-violets so that they can travel almost any distance by car. Show-plant travel by air and rail is less dependable, unless of course you are exhibiting only a few plants. Then you can pack them in a small carton, as for car transportation, and hold this yourself throughout the plane trip.

People in show business have many ways of transporting specimen plants, but I like the carton-in-carton method, and it is the one used most frequently. Each plant is placed in an individual carton that is large enough so leaves are not cramped, or several plants can be grouped in one large box. After selecting the outside container, you will need one slightly smaller for inside. Cut this one down so that the sides are 3 to 4 inches high, then turn it bottoms up. For one plant, cut a hole in the center just large enough to hold the pot snugly. If you are using a larger container for two or more plants, space them carefully on the inner box top so that foliage will not rub; then cut out the holes at appropriate locations. Pack crumpled newspaper between inner and outer boxes so that there will be no shifting.

Plants thus secured will travel well, either around the corner, across town, or several hundred miles. If your plants will be on the road overnight, take them into your hotel or motel room as soon as you stop, and open the box tops to let in air. But take care that plants are not in a draft. Check the soil of each to be sure it is still nicely moist. In case of dryness, apply room-temperature water. If you are traveling in severely cold weather, don't put plants in the car until it has been warmed up. Then be sure that no air current direct from the heater strikes them.

15

A GLANCE AT OTHER GESNERIADS

The family is one of nature's masterpieces.
Santayana

Few are the saintpaulia enthusiasts today who are satisfied to grow African-violets alone. In the past decade, many other fascinating and unique gesneriads have been made available by dealers and come into demand. Some of these are increasingly popular. A predilection for trailing plants has led me to select those that can be grown in my various hanging baskets or in the handsome birthday-present ceramic made by a skilled potter in my town. I honor this container with *Hypocyrta radicans,* in all seasons an attractive plant with pendent branches and small glossy dark green leaves. When, through the very dead of winter, it is studded with yellow-orange flowers, I feel I am growing a masterpiece. And since yellow is my favorite color, this hypocyrta is for me twice-blessed.

THE BASKET GESNERIADS

HYPOCYRTA

There are many other attractive hypocyrtas. If you are trying gesneriads for the first time, these offer an easy-to-grow start. I also like the free-flowering *H. wettsteinii,* which is less of a trailer but still

180

a basket plant if not pinched back. The shiny leaves, smaller than those of *H. radicans*, are red on the reverse, and the long-lasting waxen orange flowers show yellow lobes. I favor less *H. nummularia*, with red, black-tipped flowers, because it tends to have a late-summer dormant period when its leaves fall.

Not a trailer but semi-upright is the very interesting *H. periantho-mega*, with larger leaves and inverted greenish-yellow pouch flowers with narrow maroon stripes. The colorful calyces last long after the corolla pouches fade. Frances Batcheller, the very knowledgeable grower of gesneriads, likens these flowers to Elizabethan puffed sleeves. This is definitely a flower-show subject, and almost continuously in bloom.

Grow hypocyrtas in your usual African-violet mix with a little Sponge-Rok added for drainage if your mix seems to need it, or in the No. 2 Cornell Epiphytic Mix (Chapter 3), which some of the Gloxinia Society people swear by. Give them full sun in winter, or the brightest center location under lights, and semi-shade in summer; also fairly high humidity and a cooler spot than your African-violets enjoy. Then your hypocyrtas will bloom superbly.

COLUMNEA Goldfish-plant

Closely related to hypocyrtas, columneas have had the attention of gifted hybridizers, resulting in the Cornell Series and various handsome plants from Granger Gardens, Lyndon Lyon, and Michael Kartuz. Yellow, orange, red, or pink flowers are yours to choose, with foliage large or small, glossy or dull, even variegated. The mind really boggles when confronted with the catalogue offerings of a columnea specialist!

My grandchildren dote on what I think is *Columnea hirta*. Less long-blooming than the newer hybrids, it is a sprawling grower with brilliant orange-red flowers much-admired throughout February's four weeks. The 10-inch pot stands on a tabouret in their quite cool and sunny living-room. All visitors are required to view the "dragon flowers," for so they call them, not being reminded of goldfish at all.

Among the many glorious hybrids, I have particularly liked the popular 'Yellow Dragon', a red-rimmed lemon-yellow, and the brilliant 'Yellow Gold'. You may prefer 'Red Arrow' or the orange-red 'Early Bird'. In spring, these basket types are an arresting sight in full bloom suspended in a bay window or from a greenhouse roof. The upright growers, like the plumy 'Butterball', are also beautiful plants.

Grow columneas cooler than your saintpaulias, at 55 to 60 degrees by day and 10 degrees less at night. (The florists' cyclamen would be a good companion in this temperature range.) Let them get just a little drier than your African-violets before rewatering, and provide about the same amount of light. These also thrive in the usual soil mixture or in the Epiphytic Mix (Chapter 3). Columneas are not so well suited to fluorescent culture as are many other gesneriads.

AESCHYNANTHUS (Trichosporum)

Grow this also in the epiphytic medium. It thrives with warm nights, to 70 degrees, and seems to bloom better when somewhat potbound. Trailing and free-flowering, 'Black Pagoda', a fine Lyon hybrid, is spectacular when the clusters of orange-and-yellow flowers open along the wiry stems of marbled dark green leaves. This hybrid will generally prove more satisfactory than the species, interesting as they are. Aeschynanthus pulcher and A. parviflorus, both red flowering, are often called the lipstick-plant.

ACHIMENES   Magic-flower   Nut-orchid

Achimenes carry the gesneriad pageant into summer and may be grown for porch baskets and window boxes. They may also be planted in shaded outdoor beds. But Lyndon Lyon considers that they have a built-in time clock and that by a judicious withholding of water to induce the required four or more months of dormancy, a group of plants can be scheduled for year-round bloom. He suggests two yearly plantings of their scaly rhizomes: January first and July first, and recommends high humidity. However, this is all a tricky business for the amateur.

These are plants that must not suffer dryness or they go dormant. Even in my humid Plant Room, I sometimes have to water twice a day.

For baskets, I favor the rangy bright yellow A. flava and the branching 'Sunburst' (a George W. Park Seed Company introduction), also Lyon's 'Yellow Beauty', a fairly compact grower which really is a beauty.

One can hardly be satisfied with yellows alone in this plant of rainbow hues, whose colors almost always blend so well that I expect my 6-inch pan of an upright "mixture" to produce a most pleasant harmony. Among the compact types in other colors are Lyon's 'Crimson Beauty', salmon-pink 'Charm', and violet 'Paul Arnold', named for the international expert on achimenes.

Upper left, X Gloxinera 'Harold Hybrid'. Upper right, *Sinningia regina*. Lower left, *Sinningia speciosa* 'Emperor Wilhelm'. Lower right, *Achimenes grandiflora*. 'Emperor Wilhelm' photo by Genereux; all others, *African Violet Magazine*.

ACCENT ON FOLIAGE

EPISCIA   Peacock-plant   Flame-violet

With rich-hued foliage and various types of habit—erect branching or climbing or trailing—the episcias are desirable even without bloom, but the flowers, especially among the scarlets, are spectacular. 'Tricolor'.from Lyon makes a glorious compact, red-and-green Christmas plant; 'Velvet Brocade' from Kartuz has flowers of a lighter red and quilted foliage. Either is a handsome companion for 'Cygnet', whose glistening, fringed, white, faintly purple-spotted flowers are delightful. I am very fond of the trailing yellow episcias, particularly 'Tropical Topaz' and 'Sun Gold'. I also like 'Star of Bethlehem' with pink-starred creamy blooms.

Episcias grow well in the loose epiphytic mixture (Chapter 3) or in well-fertilized vermiculite or perlite, and flourish under fluorescents, which bring out the glowing foliage colors. They require even more light than saintpaulias to bloom well and, should be set fairly close to growth tubes. They all come from humid lowlands of tropical America, the counterpart of the East African habitat of most saintpaulias.

ALLOPLECTUS AND NAUTILOCALYX

These two gesneriads also have handsome foliage. Rich hues occur in *Alloplectus capitatus* with red-rimmed green leaves and red-and-yellow cylindrical flowers, and in *A. vittatus* with maroon leaves marked with silver midribs and similar flowers.

When I first saw *Nautilocalyx forgettii* on a label, I thought someone who couldn't remember the name was playing a joke on me. Now I know better. This is a plant that has given me great pleasure, a strong upright grower with glossy red-veined leaves and yellow blooms. Also the cream-yellow-flowered, *N. lynchii,* which has shiny dark red foliage. *N. villosus,* covered with soft white hairs, bears lovely white flowers, purple striped. The blooms of all three resemble those of episcia.

Episcias in a strawberry jar. The varieties, beginning at top and reading clockwise, include 'Chocolate Soldier' (red); 'Lilacina' or 'Fanny Haage' (lavender-blue); *E. reptans* (the 'Flame Violet' of commerce); and 'Tropical Topaz' (yellow). *African Violet Magazine,* Tinari photo.

UPRIGHT GESNERIADS

For me then the gesneriads that are most appealing—and there are so many one must be selective—are those with a plant form different from the flat rosette of African-violets, and in colors other than their predominant white, blush, pink, rose, and lavender-to-purple shades. However, when Paul Arnold presented me with *Streptocarpus* 'Constant Nymph', a *S. rexii* hybrid with a velvety foliage rosette and lavender-blue flowers, the throat striped darker, I was enchanted, even though I had saintpaulias of much the same coloring. And this gesneriad will always be a favorite.

STREPTOCARPUS   Cape-primrose

These shallow-rooted plants from Africa have a long and lovely winter flowering season, then six months of dormancy. Since they bloom in six to eight months from seed, mature plants may well be discarded or, if you prefer, divided. The color range is pink, purple, and red. There are also bicolors, and a lovely white one with rose penciling. Plants can be grown cooler than saintpaulias or the tropical episcias. They thrive at temperatures a little below 60 degrees but will accept more warmth growing in full light but no sun. Careful watering is essential to avoid rot.

BOEA AND *PETROCOSMEA*

These two have so much the same plant form as saintpaulia that they are hardly to be included in a small mixed collection, although both make pretty pot plants. *Boea hygroscopia* with its flat leaves and purple blooms has even been mistaken for the African-violet. *Petrocosmea kerrii*, similar in growth pattern, bears yellow-marked or cream-colored flowers, and it is these that have so tantalized hybridizers with hopes of a yellow saintpaulia, but so far their efforts have been unsuccessful.

SINNINGIA

Most familiar in this group is *Sinningia speciosa,* the florist's gloxinia, a big showy plant that takes up a lot of window-sill or bench room. Through the years smaller plants have been developed and the color range increased beyond the original purple to include white, wonderful reds, pink, lavender, and two-toned flowers. American hybridizers have produced more graceful flowers and also double

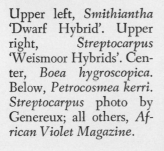

Upper left, *Smithiantha* 'Dwarf Hybrid'. Upper right, *Streptocarpus* 'Weismoor Hybrids'. Center, *Boea hygroscopica*. Below, *Petrocosmea kerri*. *Streptocarpus* photo by Genereux; all others, *African Violet Magazine*.

forms. The smaller-leaved slipper type is a favorite. Miniature forms are exciting and fun to grow. (More about these last in Chapter 16.)

Gloxinias require more light than saintpaulias and a somewhat cooler atmosphere, 65 to 70 degrees. They need protection from strong sun and a warm humid atmosphere in growing season. Fluorescent light is desirable and particularly when tubers are just starting into growth. The dormant period requires careful handling. Cease watering as flowering ceases. And never wet the leaves, as they are very prone to rot.

Two white species are more appealing to me, than the old S. *speciosa*. The comely S. *eumorpha,* reaching 4 feet, shows purple markings inside the pendent corolla. Fragrance distinguishes the flowers of S. *tubiflora*—a sweetness like that of orange blossoms. This one is so light-demanding it is rarely successful even under fluorescents; it fact, it is more likely to bloom in full summer sun if put outdoors. It is not the easiest of the sinningias but one of the most exciting. Gloxinias, like saintpaulias, can be propagated from leaf cuttings.

RECHSTEINERIA

If this tuberous-rooted genus had a nice common name, it would probably be one of the most popular gesneriads for it is easier to grow than most of them. If tubers are mature, R. *cardinalis* can be brought into bloom at any time, and as a Christmas plant rivals the poinsettia. Bright red tubular hooded flowers develop in clusters at the terminal of each stalk, and they last well. For December display, pot late in August, leaving the tubers partly exposed; or sow seed the first of May. R. *verticillata,* the "double-decker plant," bears pink flowers, purple spotted, above three-whorled leaves. Its value in a collection of gesneriads lies in the contrast of its growth pattern to that of the other plants.

GLOXINERA   (X Gloxinera)

Because of the close relationship of *Sinningia* to *Rechsteineria,* many crosses have been made and produced hybrids in a wide color range. You might like the salmon 'Clarice' or lilac 'Edith M' among the fairly large ones—to 30 inches in 6-inch pots. The pink 'Rita L' is a handsome smaller-growing gloxinera. To many people the minia-

tures from the crosses are the most appealing, and the next chapter
tells about these small charmers.

SMITHIANTHA   Temple-bells

From late summer to early winter, the smithianthas will bring color
to a spacious plant room or greenhouse, opening their tubular flowers,
flaring at the tip, in a bright red-orange-yellow range. Many are tall
growers—even above three feet when in bloom. They thrive in full
winter sun but in summer, morning sun only. For under fluorescents,
it is best to select the easy-to-grow white-flowered S. *multiflora* with a
yellow throat spotted red and giving an overall effect of yellow. It
grows to 2 feet. There are a number of dwarf hybrid smithianthas
(sometimes sold as *Naegelia*). Set these as close as an inch or two
from the lights in their first stages, moving them lower as the tops
develop. Plant the scaly rhizomes in May or June after they have had
the required three to four months of dormancy, setting each of the
dwarfs in a 3-inch pot. Plants will grow for about twelve weeks before
starting to bloom at the top.

The species are interesting, particularly the red-orange flowered,
red-velvety-leaved S. *cinnabarina*. The hybrids of the Cornell Series
are spectacular large plants, up to 5 feet. They have been imagina-
tively named, with reference to the popular name of the genus. Five
green-leaved cultivars are 'Abbey', 'Cathedral', 'Cloister', 'Matins',
and 'Vespers'. Red-leaved varieties carry names of the early California
missions: 'Capistrano', 'Carmel', 'San Gabriel', 'Santa Barbara', and
'Santa Clara'. And what's in a clever name? Often it assures the popularity of a plant.

KOHLERIA   (Isoloma, Tydaea)

Also growing from scaly rhizomes, these upright plants bear flowers
of gracefully swelling tube shape with spreading lobes at the tip, in
contrast to the narrower funnel form of smithiantha. K. *eriantha* may
grow to 4 feet, with vermilion flowers. K. *amabilis* is lower-growing
and long-blooming, with green-and-magenta-pink flowers, a good
choice when your window sills are running over and you want a
basket plant. Perhaps the hybrids are the most appealing, especially
the Kartuz red-spotted yellow 'Carnival', rose-pink 'Princess', and
Frances Batcheller's 'Rongo', with marbled foliage and large pink
flowers darkly spotted. Good light and generous feeding are required,

particularly at the start of growth after dormancy when legginess needs to be discouraged.

These then are some of the very delightful African-violet cousins, relatives you will probably like to live with. They are so diversified in plant and flower forms, in texture and color of foliage, in seasons of bloom, that they are extremely tempting. And, as saintpaulia enthusiasts readily admit, "I can resist anything but temptation!"

Kohleria amabilis in a hanging basket. A gay abundance of red-spotted pink flowers is set off by silvery sage-green leaves with brown markings. *African Violet Magazine* photo.

16

MAXI PLEASURE FROM THE MINIS

Trifles make perfection, and perfection is no trifle.
Michelangelo

The first time I handled miniature African-violets I had the same sinking feeling as when I bathed my brand-new grandchild for the first time. Both plants and baby seemed to me alarmingly fragile, and I felt clumsy and frightened. But experience and time have encouraged me so that now I am fairly equal to both plants and child and, of course, I dote on both. I suppose all women are drawn to small things—puppies, kittens, infants, and also miniature plants. Certainly these tiny saintpaulias and other gesneriads are an endearing group, and the plants my visitors always admire most. In fact, the minis are so attractive I foresee a new kind of addiction (if I may use that word in a decent context) among houseplant enthusiasts generally and smitten African-violet fans in particular. My table-top fixture set on a pine chest in a "passage room" without windows lights fifteen miniatures, and they look so pretty there, my progress through the house is inevitably delayed, for I must always linger a moment to admire.

SAINTPAULIA MINIATURES

These small-fry African-violets are a lot of fun, and under fluorescent lights most of them produce a succession of charming jewel blossoms. I am not sure, however, that the miniatures require as much light as the standard types, although others have found they needed more, even "twice as much." On a shelf under a long lamp I elevated some plants on inverted pots to within 3 inches of the light; there some bloomed acceptably, others bunched, and they were purples, not pinks or whites. Individualists no doubt!

Anyway a number of my little charmers also bloom well in winter at sunny uncurtained south windows, and in summer at north windows. Each is set in its own curved yellow Japanese dish, and reflection from the yellow probably increases the effect of the natural light. So grouped, the little ones are decorative, and an amusing contrast to the standard plants on the same broad window sill. I let down the Venetian blind at night as protection from cold although the windows are already covered by storm sash.

Culture of the miniatures is not much different from that of the larger plants. The soil mixture is the same but could perhaps be a little more porous and open with additional perlite or Sponge-Rok. I water the small plants as I do the large ones, with warm water to which very weak fertilizer is always added, except for a few days each month when I pour plain water over the top soil to avoid an accumulation of fertilizer salts. If you find watering from your long-spouted can difficult so that you incline to overwater, use an atomizer spray like the ones for window cleaning. I mist my plants regularly with my trusty "fogger," regularly meaning when I have time, which isn't always every day, but humidity stays above 40 percent and temperature at about 72 degrees.

My plants are in 2¼-inch pots, and I do not think miniatures need pots much larger, certainly not beyond 2½'s, but some of the old soil should be replaced with a fresh mixture every eight months or so.

ORIGINS

Lyndon Lyon has hybridized a number of saintpaulia miniatures and in the full color range. Just now he is bent on producing trailers, and I can imagine no more enchanting plants than tiny blooming miniatures in little hanging baskets. Lyndon expects his new plants to come from those seedling miniatures of trailers that have a pink-star-type saintpaulia for one parent.

In his breeding for miniatures, he has used these five species: S. *grotei*, S. *magungensis*, S. *nitida*, S. *orbicularis*, and S. *shumensis*. This last is probably a common ancestor of all the tiny saintpaulias. It has rounded leaves and bluish-white blooms. You may enjoy growing this little species, especially if you are hybridizing for miniatures. (A picture of S. *shumensis* appears in Chapter 9.) Be more than careful about overwatering this one, since it comes from dry places. And it is definitely a multiple-crown grower. Rather than letting those suckers be a bother, give this one, as growth indicates, a larger pot than the others and let it expand freely and naturally.

Regarding his own hybridizing, Lyndon writes: "By using the newly-developed miniatures like 'Tiny Pink' and 'Edith's Toy', any of the saintpaulia species can be miniaturized *in one generation*. To accomplish this, several hundred seeds from the crosses are sown and when the seedlings are big enough to pot, search is made for green 'vases,' a growth form smaller than and different from that of a standard seedling. These are put back in the seedling dishes, where small plants develop from the 'bulbous ends' of the 'vases,' and most of these will be miniatures."

It is obvious that we are going to be offered almost as extensive an array of miniature saintpaulias as we already have of standard cultivars. Even now, almost at the start, there are many more excellent ones listed in catalogues than I can mention here.

What to plant a crop of miniatures in? Those thin lightweight thumb pots Lyndon Lyon ships his plants in are treasures to be saved, and they can be cut to squatty size with small tin snips to fit into "ivy bowls," brandy snifters, or those little covered glass bowls that come at Christmas with greens and red berries. My 'Tiny Blue' on the breakfast table is a delight in one of these. When you cut down the thumb pots, go round and round as if you were peeling an apple. Don't cut down or you will split the pots as I did on my first two tries. A hacksaw blade without the handle is also a good tool for the purpose. Some collectors plant in demitasse cups, but drainage holes in these must be most delicately drilled to avoid shattering the cups. (Careful husbands have successfully managed this.)

Ruth Katzenberger contrives little "greenhouses" in which to develop choice specimens. "Overpot each plant," she says, "in a 3½-inch squatty pot with plenty of crocking. Bring soil up to the lower edge of the pot rim, and insert the plant. Pierce three holes in the bottom of a clear plastic drinking cup (these for circulation of air), and invert the cup over the plant. It will just fit inside the pot rim and so make an individual greenhouse. The nice part about this method is that pods may be permitted to form and break open right there. The seed will germinate around the plant, and you can pick out seedlings as soon as they are large enough to handle. It is also easy to remove the specimen plant for use in an arrangement at a flower show."

OTHER MINIATURE GESNERIADS

Unlike African-violets, many other miniature gesneriads do not readily hybridize. Furthermore, most of the new miniatures are sterile and must be propagated vegetatively. On that account there are not nearly so many; in fact, it has taken about a decade to obtain the few that are available. Sometimes, however, miniatures in the home do produce a seed pod, and plants are easy to grow from seed. Mrs. Wright tells of her experience with a ripe pod from *Gloxinera* 'Pink Petite'. She sowed the seed over a mixture of peat and vermiculite, covered the pot with Saran Wrap, and placed it in a bathroom window. In a little more than two weeks, tiny plants were in evidence, and in a month she had 'Pink Petite' "all over the house."

SINNINGIAS AND GLOXINERAS

The small sinningias are the easiest to obtain, including the two species, S. *concinna* and S. *pusilla,* plus their hybrids. The variable wine-to-orchid-to-almost-white 'Wood Nymph', with an edging or dotted throat on blooms of different forms, is a cross between them; a third generation backcross produced 'Bright Eyes', and these two are different enough for you to want both.

Other hybrids produced with these two species have involved a much larger plant. Most popular because of their ease of culture are Mrs. Katzenberger's lilac-and-white 'Dollbaby', a cross of the lavender S. *pusilla* with the white S. *eumorpha,* and 'Dollbaby's' counterpart, 'Cindy', a first-generation from S. *concinna* with S. *eumorpha,* the flower picking up the purple concinna spots and elongating them into stripes. ('Cindy' comes from a cross made by Dr. Thomas E. Talpey, an electrical genius, who built the receiving set for our interplanetary radar set in Arecibo, Puerto Rico. Like many other important people, he is interested in gesneriads.) 'White Sprite' is a sport of S. *pusilla,* and 'Snowflake', a chemically induced mutation from it. 'Freckles', with blossoms of the S. *concinna* type, is choice and easy to grow. Fisher's 'Tom Thumb' is a true miniature of the florist's gloxinia (*Sinningia speciosa*), a delightful diminutive, red with a white-bordered corolla, a nice contrast to the pastels.

Intergeneric crosses between Sinningia and Rechsteineria provide pink flowers in this group of miniature tuberous gesneriads. Often offered as a pink 'Dollbaby' is 'Dollbaby's' progeny, correctly called *Gloxinera* 'Cupid's Doll', but this is not the true pink of such gloxineras as 'Pink Petite', 'Ramadeva', or 'Krishna', these being also smaller.

OTHER GROWTH TYPES

Forms different from the familiar rosette occur among miniature gesneriads. The lovely *Koellikeria erinoides* sends up racemes of tiny pink-and-white flowers that reach well above the pale green silver-splashed leaves. It grows not from a tuberous root but from a scaly rhizome.

The diastemas offer five more upright growers from scaly rhizomes. *Diastema vexans* with dark-spotted white flowers is the most widely cultivated. It reaches to four inches, and makes a pretty picture when several are grown in a tiny basket, which sets off the branching stems.

There are other minute gesneriads, but few are readily available. Some, like the little *Streptocarpus*, are necessarily grown as annuals and propagated from seed each time. These are a challenge to dedicated growers, since the seed quickly loses viability.

NOTES ON CULTURE

While all the miniatures can be grown uncovered, fine specimen plants are more likely to result from the extra humidity provided by jars, bottles, and other glass containers with or without covers. A large fish tank set up as a scene with several of the little ones makes a healthy and attractive setting. (This is the Wardian-case way.) Hills and valleys, rocks, and a mirror pond, can be suggested with both "tall" and rosette types. Under these conditions those with rhizomes multiply so rapidly that their growth must be controlled to keep them from taking over. If you cover the container with a sheet of plastic or glass and water drops collect, lift and wipe it and slide it a little to the side for a while every day so plants can have an airing.

Watering miniatures can be tricky; it is so easy to drown the tiny root systems. In glass bowls or terrariums, provide a foundation of stones, perlite, or sand to take care of excess when you have been heavy-handed. Watering with an atomizer spray is a safe method. But if you ever do swamp the plants, use your meat-baster to draw off

water. Of course, these small gesneriads must never dry out completely. The tiny tubers and rhizomes have little storage space and if
they get too dry, they will go into dormancy. If this happens just
before a show, it could ruin what might have won a blue ribbon.

With saintpaulias true dormancy does not occur with all the leaves
dying off and only the rootstock left. But dormancy is a phase of the
life cycle of most tuberous and rhizomatous gesneriads. However, well-
grown miniature sinningias and gloxineras are unlikely to go dormant
unless you induce dormancy with too little water. If plants do get too
dry and begin to go dormant, they will not grow well again in the
same cycle, no matter what you do after this reaction has set in.

Removing the crown will also cause dormancy. In either case, the
tuber will rest a short time and then send up a new shoot. Sometimes
a crown that has been growing for a long time becomes unsightly. If
this occurs, remove it to force new growth. This may happen with
'Dollbaby', which will begin to send out several crowns as the tuber
matures; each one can be rooted to get more flowering plants quickly.
To remove leaves or spent blossom stems, cut with sharp manicure
scissors, for the slightest pull is likely to uproot the whole plant.

17

A CHAPTER OF HORRORS—PEST AND DISEASE

The faintest streak that on a petal lies
May speak instruction to initiate eyes.
William Cullen Bryant

Hearing people talk at conventions and club meetings, you'd think the African-violet was the world's problem plant. I can assure you that it is not. If you stick to sterilized soil, provide a proper environment, and maybe just maybe, spray with an all-purpose African-violet insecticide once a month or so, you aren't going to run into trouble. I don't. A happy plant like a happy child stays healthy. One collector with some 200 plants reports that in *seven years* only two of them were attacked by mealy bug, three by crown rot, and two by mite.

Of course, she isolates new plants from any source for six to eight weeks, giving latent trouble plenty of time to show up. During this trial period, she keeps one watering pot just for the strangers and washes her hands before she tends her other plants, not wishing to be a Typhoid Mary! Also, though an enthusiastic gardener, she never brings thrip-prone delphinium or gladiolus into the house near her African-violets.

Now before you get scared stiff by what follows and begin doing things to your plants which they don't need (and diagnosing ailments which aren't there, like new medical students reading about diseases), glance at Figures 35 and 36. One look will probably be worth more information than the thousand "tells" that follow.

In dealing with this gruesome subject, to which Bernard Greeson has brought me so much light—see his Quick Reference Trouble Chart at the end of this chapter—I want to emphasize *prevention* rather than cures, because in some cases there really are no cures as yet.

Let's start with nematodes; they *can* be prevented, and mites as well. These two are the worst. But first a word about insecticides.

TYPES OF INSECTICIDES

There are three types. *Stomach poisons,* sprayed on plants, act when insects eat foliage. *Contact insecticides* destroy by touching adult or newly hatched insects, larvae, and eggs. Kelthane, Malathion 50, and Lindane are examples, some having both effects; all give a fast kill, and are also preventives if regularly applied. *Systemic* insecticides, dry or wet, are slower but their effect lasts longer, better for prevention than clean up.

The Shell Vapona insect strip (available at Shell Oil gas stations and at some grocery stores) is a marvelously effective odorless fumigant to hang with your plants. The gold strip looks like an ornament, and for three months in the Plant Room, has given protection against aphids, whiteflies, mealy bugs, thrips, and mites in crowns. It eradicated scale and mealy bugs when a strip was enclosed in a large plastic bag with a plant. If you do this, take care that the strip hangs well above, not touching, the plant. Also available at grocery stores is Raid House and Garden Bug Killer, safe on saintpaulias and easy to use.

NEMATODES, Root (No. 1 killer)

Symptoms. Loss of vigor and general debility in a plant may be ascribed to starvation, over- or under-watering, too much or too little light, or the wrong fertilizer. However, if foliage loses its good green color, becomes pale and dull, and outer leaves droop, if young leaves emerge already damaged and sustain the injury through life, if flowers are fewer and those borne have a lackluster look, if there has been a procession of other ills—mealy bugs, black flies, springtails, or some such—if the low center of plant stalk feels soft and the plant seems rocky or loose in the pot, if several or all of these conditions occur, you may as well prepare yourself for the worst and turn the sufferer out of the pot so that you can examine roots. Small pulpy enlargements, swellings to two or three times normal diameters (rather than knots), these and a galled spongy condition of the stalk at the soil line, or an enlarged rough and calloused stem (signs of resistance to trouble) fill in but one picture, as in Figure 36.

Diagnosis. Root-nematode is indicated, the hated fifth columnist of saintpaulias. The fine, threadlike, transparent worms destroy indirectly by interfering with life processes. The trouble may appear to be root or crown rot. Because diagnosis is difficult, plants are often first treated for other ills, and many eventually die.

Damage is mostly done by females migrating through soil to rootlets. Tissue is pierced and entry made to the very center. Then they become sedentary, feed, and grow, remaining for life in the one spot. Nematodes inject a secretion that causes plant cells to enlarge and become nectarial. These cells produce food for larvae, which become adult in three to four weeks. Each female lays some 400 eggs that create more nectarial cells in the same place or not far away.

With a razor blade, slice through a stem near a rotted area; examine it under a hand lens; you will probably find pearly dots. These are the root nematodes. Examining the whole area with the lens, you will see that the stem covering has been stripped off and that a brown moist area encircles it. You may see fungus gnats, reddish mites, wiggle tails, and tiny garden centipedes, all profiting by the damage done but not the primary cause of it.

Nematodes interfere with the circulatory system. When a plant resists stoppage, roots swell to keep passages open, therefore the rough thickened stems.

What to Do. Plant only in sterilized soil (see "Soil Purification" in Chapter 3). There is no cure, at present. If your plants are in bad condition, by all means discard them, dumping all soil into the garbage can (never on the compost pile), and sterilizing pots before using them again. Since nematodes travel in water flowing out of pots and can be carried on the spout of a watering can, in soil, on pebbles in plant trays, even on your fingers, *you can't be too careful.*

NEMATODES, Foliar

Symptoms. Centers seem to stop growing; veins appear swollen, stems also, particularly at the base. Lower leaves may show triangular spotting. It's difficult to pin down the trouble because these same conditions can indicate other troubles.

Diagnosis. Probably foliar nematodes.

What to do. Scratch a granular sodium selenate systemic into the top soil. Water it in well. Roots will absorb it, send it through the top of the plant, and feeding nematodes will be poisoned. (You will also be checking possible mites with this treatment.) Use the milder sodium selenate, P-40 (a miticide, available in small quantities).

In a Greenhouse. To fumigate quantities of soil apply Dowfume MC-2 (methyl bromide). You need an applicator, some length of polyethylene tubing and plastic sheeting. Attach the applicator to the can, along with the tubing. Cover the soil with the sheeting so that it is gas proof. Run the tubing under the mass of soil and let the gas do the work. Aerate soil for about a week after fumigation. Wear a mask while you do this.

MITES (No. 2 killer)

Three kinds, too minute to be visible, attack African-violets. Evidence varies with each but controls and preventives are the same.

Symptoms. In the early stages of an attack, foliage in the center of the crown looks lighter than the rest. The smaller leaves may be a sickly gray or yellowish green. Buds, blossoms, and blossom stems are distorted. These last may thicken abnormally or be considerably shorter than usual. Growth in general is dwarfed and centers bunched. Hairiness is more pronounced. Buds may drop prematurely. In later stages, the central crown will have been destroyed and new "desperation" growth will be pushing out at the side of the center (Figure 36).

Diagnosis. If leaves tend to cup *upward* and are quite brittle, this is probably *cyclamen mite* (a cousin of the spider family). If leaves curl down, it's more likely to be *broad mite,* which is easier to clean up. If silky cobwebs stretch from leaf to leaf or cover flowers, and foliage is gray, reddish-brown, mottled, or speckled, it's probably *red spider mite.* If you look into the convolutions of the smallest leaves, you may detect egg masses. Young plants will be hurt more than older plants that have the reserve of strong outer leaves on which mites cannot subsist. If both cyclamen and broad mites are present, and they may be, you will see some darting about much faster than others. They are the broad mites.

But keep in mind that excessive fertilizer may also cause distortion; if this is the trouble, flush it out by watering heavily three times within an hour. Or plants grown too close to fluorescent lights or exposed for too many hours may develop bunched centers, particularly

FIGURES 35–36

PESTS AND DISEASES

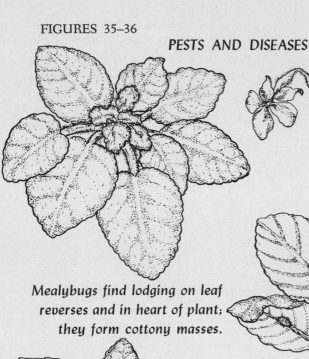

Cyclamen mite causes young center leaves to be malformed and unusually hairy. Flowers, if any, will be discolored, stalks misshaped.

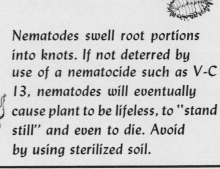

Mealybugs find lodging on leaf reverses and in heart of plant; they form cottony masses.

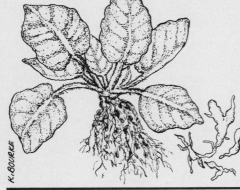

K. BOURKE

Nematodes swell root portions into knots. If not deterred by use of a nematocide such as V-C 13, nematodes will eventually cause plant to be lifeless, to "stand still" and even to die. Avoid by using sterilized soil.

CONTROL MEASURES

When used regularly, aerosols prepared for violets help control pests. Read labels carefully.

Small attacks of mealybugs may be halted by touching each insect with cotton dipped in alcohol.

202

Crown rot may cause plant to wilt, the outer leaves drooping over the pot. Watering will not revive it. Usually the plant can be saved by removing from pot, washing root system and cutting away all discolored tissue. Paint cut areas with fungicide, then repot in sterilized soil.

Petiole rot causes older leaves to become jellylike where they droop over and touch the sides of the pot. Caused by fertilizer salts on soil surface and pot rim. Remove affected leaves. Top watering helps avoid this trouble.

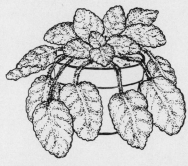

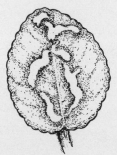

Ring spot on upper surfaces of violet leaves is caused by watering or spraying with water of a temperature varying more than 10 degrees from that of the room in which the plants are growing. Hot sun on wet foliage also causes ring spot.

K. BOURKE

In case of serious insect attack, dip plants in lukewarm pesticide. Plastic collar holds soil in place.

Apply chemicals through V-shaped hole in soil; keep off foliage.

203

African-violets with pale leaves, which usually do better placed at the ends of the tubes. (See Chapter 5.)

What to Do. If it's mites, act fast. They reproduce at a terrible rate: according to one estimate 200,000,000 in three months! Apply a contact spray, Kelthane, 50% Malathion, or Cythion would be a good sequence with an occasional substitution of Dimite (in case the mites are developing immunity to any one insecticide). Or apply a systemic to the soil.

In any case, it will take a few weeks to clean up a light infestation, and even at that it may be about two months before plants are well recovered—and look it. All of your plants may not be infested. Mite is unlikely to travel to pots kept 3 inches apart, nor will it live on a window sill or other surface away from plant tissues for twenty-four hours. If one part of your collection is still mite-free, take every pre-caution to keep it so. Segregate the suspect violets, and use water from a vessel kept just for them. Wash your hands before touching other plants. Since mites spread by contact, let me repeat, be sure *you* are not the carrier.

Contact insecticides may be used as a spray or dip. Follow container directions; usually 1 teaspoon of a miticide to 1 gallon of lukewarm water, *mixed well,* gives good results. If you spray, put plants in a bathtub and spray forcefully and thoroughly, reaching the deep center of the crowns, as well as both upper and under leaf surfaces. If neces-sary, remove a few leaves to open up tight center areas to the spray.

For the dip, mix the solution in a vessel large enough for the plant to be entirely submerged. Cover the soil with a plastic collar. Even so if you are treating a number of plants, the solution may get too dirty to do the whole lot in one mixture. You will then have to prepare more than one batch of dip.

Let sprayed or dipped plants dry in a shaded place before returning them to direct light. If too many particles of soil adhere to foliage, spray lightly with clear lukewarm water right after the dip.

Repeat the dip or spray in seven to ten days until you have given three clean-up treatments. Then spray or dip once a month as part of your program of preventive care. And please, while you are spraying or dipping, protect your hands and arms by wearing long rubber gloves.

Reconditioning. Plants that have suffered mite damage have a very sick look indeed, even after mites have been dispatched. Usually damaged tissue is even more damaged by the rigors of dipping or spraying. A breaking or wilting point may develop low down on petioles so that many large leaves fall. You cannot help this, so be philosophic, knowing that the alternative was probably the loss of the infected plant. With tweezers, pick out the wilted center leaves. Remove others that are severely damaged or distorted, but don't remove *all* the foliage until some new appears. Plants breathe through their leaves and even impaired ones are better than none. Suckers will appear at the side of the old crown. Select one to train toward the center to make a new crown. Cut off the others.

When the plant seems convalescent and well on the way to new life, repot it. Cut off dead or brown roots. These were not directly attacked by the mite, but have reacted to the general illness. Use a clean pot (disinfect clay by dipping in boiling water; wash plastic, if it was used before, in soapy water and dip in a disinfectant solution), and probably a smaller one, since the root system is now likely to be considerably reduced. Set the plant a little farther down in the soil than it was originally to conceal the lower bareness of the new sucker you are training. Withhold plant food and grow on the dry side until complete recovery is assured and the shock of transplanting absorbed.

Prevention. To be on the safe side, spray plants monthly with a miticide, or apply a systemic to the soil to get mite protection for three to six months. By all means, add a systemic to any soil mixture you prepare yourself.

STUNT

Symptoms. Similar to those of cyclamen mite. Leaves are shorter and broader than normal ones of a given variety. They appear thickened, quite turgid and brittle. The marginal crenations are obliterated or reduced. The margins are rolled up, exposing the usually lighter green lower surface. Younger leaves seem more affected than older ones. All look shinier because the length of the hairs has been reduced two-thirds. Petioles are shorter.

Diagnosis. All this adds up to a pathological condition called Stunt. It disfigures, but does not necessarily destroy.

What to Do. This is a virus disease for which there is no cure. Plants must be discarded, since stunt persists in the progeny of affected plants propagated by leaf cuttings or divisions. Before parting with a choice specimen, however, be sure it is not just another victim of cyclamen mite, fertilizer burn, or too much fluorescent light. See what results are possible with one of the treatments for mite, or if the effects of fertilizer burn and light are eliminated. If growth becomes normal again, rejoice. Otherwise burn the plant.

Prevention. Wise and regular care will go far to prevent stunt unless you have been unfortunate enough to get plants of diseased parentage.

APHIDS OR PLANT LICE

Symptoms. Clusters of tiny, usually black or green, insects on succulent new growth.

Diagnosis. Very likely these are aphids or plant lice that debilitate by sucking out vital juices.

What to Do. If the attack is light and only just starting, spray on three successive days with lukewarm water, or hold the plant on its side under a slow-running faucet, carefully turning so that the stream of water cleanses all the affected growth. If the attack is severe and the plant is simply crawling, an unlikely condition unless other affairs of life have prevented regular care and inspection, as they sometimes must, spray or dip plants in a solution of Malathion 50 or Cythion, or spray thoroughly with Raid House and Garden Bug Killer, which is safe for saintpaulias.

Prevention. Spray regularly once a month with your favorite all-purpose product. Then you will very likely never have aphids—or mealy bugs either. There is evidence that mites too are thus deterred. Treating soil with a systemic—primarily for mites—also discourages aphids.

BLACK FLIES

Symptoms. Tiny flies or gnats swarm around plants.

Diagnosis. These are fungus gnats.

What to Do. To get rid of the flies, which are apparently only a nuisance, spray with a general insecticide or your all-purpose aerosol. Raid House and Garden Bug Killer usually finishes them off. But since these flies lay eggs in the soil and on any rotting leaves in trays or saucers and the hatching larvae feed on fine root hairs, a soil drench may be in order. You could use Terraclor or P-40.

MEALY BUG (above ground)

Symptoms. Plants look dusty. Flower stems and leaves have a grayish, webby appearance. Deep in the crown and on the underside of leaves, cottony clusters will be visible (Figure 36).

Diagnosis. This is mealy bug, which usually moves in on plants ailing from some other cause, although it may appear on healthy plants, too. It exhausts and, if not eliminated, destroys plants by extracting cell sap through sucking mouth parts.

What to Do. Single-crown plants are more easily cleaned up than multiple-crown specimens, which offer just that many more hiding places. In light attacks, apply an alcohol-dipped swab or small paintbrush to the mealy bugs and also gently rub the spot where they have been. Inspect and treat a plant every few days until all the newly-hatched offenders have been destroyed. After applying alcohol, hold each plant on its side under a slow-running faucet of warm water. This will wash off excess alcohol, which has a dangerously drying effect on the tissues of the brittle stems and leaves.

Severe attacks require sterner measures. To reach safely all foliage folds, dip plants in a solution of Malathion 50 or Cythion, as you do for cyclamen mite. Cythion is a form of malathion with a broader spectrum of insect kill without the smell that some people object to in Malathion 50. Or apply a granular systemic like P-40 (AV Miticide).

Prevention. Monthly spraying with an insecticide deters mealy bug. Since badly infested plants may have to be discarded, try to *avoid* rather than to have to eradicate mealy bug. Watch out for contamination from gift plants or other houseplants that may carry mealy bug. It can also be air-borne from shrubbery outside an open window.

SOIL MEALY BUG

Symptoms. The plant wilts, as if suffering from crown or root rot; limp leaves are dull and have no luster. Infested plants may become small in the center. Although blossoms may appear at first, buds cease to form as the infestation gains a hold.

Diagnosis. This is soil mealy bug, a fairly new cause of grief, especially in southern California and other warm climates. Where conditions are suitable, soil mealy bugs occur in great numbers, working on the roots. The insect is about $\frac{1}{16}$th of an inch long, and easily seen under a magnifying glass. It has six legs on a slim body coated with firm white wax and looks more like a particle of perlite or Sponge-Rok than the cottony white mealy bug which attacks foliage.

Soil mealy bugs eat root tips, making it impossible for a plant to take up moisture or nutrients from the soil. Heavy watering to revive wilted plants suffering from an infestation only aggravates the condition and leads to fatal rotting of roots. If you suspect soil mealy bugs, examine the rootball in strong light. If present, the grayish white bugs will be crawling over the surface. The cottony masses of eggs that we associate with common mealy bugs are not likely to be seen at first, as they are usually inside the rootball. Sometimes soil mealy bugs can be detected on the surface of the soil around the base of a plant, or in the saucer below immediately after watering.

What to Do. As a clean-up, scratch Dr. "V" in the top soil of each plant, about ¼ teaspoon to a 3-inch pot. Repeat application in three to six months as required.

Prevention. Use only sterilized potting soil. Inspect every rootball at transplanting-time. Isolate newcomers. Soil mealy bugs travel from pot to pot, usually as water drains away and takes a bug with it to the tray below. Therefore it is doubly wise to drench gravel, sand, or any other medium on which pots stand, with something like Dr. "V". Also, African-violets treated with a sodium selenate product as a mite deterrent are not likely to be bothered by soil mealy bug. Isotox Systemic Granules, mixed in the potting soil, is another possibility, safer and generally available at garden shops.

THRIPS

Symptoms. Whitish spots appear on leaves, also blotches and dead areas along the edges. There may be wilting or falling of leaves, perhaps some small reddish specks. On blooms you may see white streaks, particularly noticeable on darker varieties. There will be malformations and premature bud and bloom fall. If you remove and pull apart a few flowers (not just one), you may see tiny swift-moving insects. Some fallen flowers may show a pin-point opening in the anthers. Flick a few of these, and you can watch the culprits emerge.

Diagnosis. Consider all factors. Bud and bloom drop may result from low humidity, gas in the atmosphere, or too little fresh air. Leaf blotching may also occur from a number of causes, but add petal streaking to those (don't judge on streaking alone; this can be a normal reaction to radical seasonal changes, especially in autumn), and the answer probably is thrips.

If you hold a hand lens over one of these small active pests long enough to examine one, you will see that it is gray, brown, or black, with two pairs of wings fringed with hairs. In all it is about as "thick as a thin needle and as long as a hyphen." Rasping, sucking mouth parts do the damage. Thrips scrape away surface tissues so as to dine upon the juices of leaf or flower. The dead walls of the broken cells first turn white, then rusty, as deterioration spreads. The reddish specks you see, which later turn black, are excrement.

Where do thrips come from? It is hard to say, but very likely from cut flowers or from other plants, such as amaryllis, gladiolus, or gloxinia, or from an infested African-violet added to your collection.

What to Do. Spray or dip as for aphids, being sure that the solution drips down onto the soil to catch any young thrips which may be there. Shade the plant for three days and be on watch. Pinching off buds and flowers—if you can bear to do it—is an heroic measure. This, with spraying, will get rid of a multitude of thrips, when you don't want to engage in drastic dipping.

Prevention. Use sterilized soil with a granular miticide added; have a regular spray program, perhaps with Raid, to deter the enemy (and be sure to reach the top soil so as to catch the nymphs); isolate newcomers till you are sure they are in health.

CROWN ROT

Symptoms. A previously healthy plant flops, the long outer leaves droop over the edge of the pot. Watering will not revive it, though it appears to be simply wilted. Actually it may be suffering from over-watering, particularly if the condition develops in the fall or spring. Or the sections of a plant you have just divided may go limp, as in Figure 37. Again watering will not arrest the decline.

Diagnosis. This may be crown rot, perhaps due to irregular care, resulting in desert-to-swamp conditions, under which unfriendly fungus organisms thrive. These are present in most fertile soils, but are controlled by good culture. In the case of division, the fungus enters at an area of bruised or cut tissue.

What to do. Try to reroot your plant. Remove it from the pot, shake off the soil, and do a thorough pruning job. Remove any dead roots or soft stem. Cut right back to firm healthy, green or white tissue, even if you must sacrifice a lot of growth. Paint the cut areas with sulfur, Fermate, or other fungicide. Then plant the remains in peat and vermiculite, sand, perlite, or soil, or support the top so that the base reaches a steady supply of water, as in a narrow-necked vase. Unless the crown rot was caused by nematodes, your plant will probably survive. (If it starts to grow and then flops, you may safely diagnose nematodes, and had better burn the plant.)

Prevention. Be regular in care and mindful of overwatering, and also of too deep planting. Simple crown rot is easily avoided. Avoid letting water or spray material seep down and settle in the crown of a plant. If you water from below or through a V-shaped hole in the soil, you will lessen danger. When dividing plants, or when cutting them back for rerooting, take the precaution of applying to all cut areas sulfur, Fermate, or some other good fungicide. Also grow divisions on the dry side until they take hold.

PETIOLE ROT OR EFFLORESCENCE DISEASE

Symptoms. Leaf stalks particularly of older leaves become jelly-like where they droop over and touch the side of the pot, as in Figure 35. You may find an orange-brown or rust-colored lesion at the point where the petiole touches the pot rim or lies in contact with soil. Some stalks may already have shriveled and collapsed. (This petiole rot is not to be confused with the normal discarding by a plant of its oldest, most mature leaves. With these there is a *gradual* yellowing and withering, actually a ripening.)

Diagnosis. Petiole or leaf-stalk rot is a chemical injury, called "efflorescence disease." It is apparently caused by contact of leaf stalks with fertilizer salts that collect on the surface of the soil and on the rim of the pot.

Cure. Get rid of the incrustation as quickly as possible. Remove any affected leaves, cutting as far down on the stem as you can. Flush the soil with heavy waterings, about three times in one hour will do it. Stir the top soil slightly with a fork. Then repot in a clean container of the same size. Thereafter for a few weeks use country rain water, boiled water that has been cooled, or distilled water.

Prevention. Good culture will minimize this trouble by keeping petioles sturdy and so, in most varieties, held *above* pot rims. Top watering will also keep fertilizer salts flushed down into the soil where they belong. (The V-shaped hole in the soil for occasional or regular top watering is an excellent device.) Avoid overuse of fertilizer, particularly from below. Be watchful of any damaged petioles especially on plants in plastic or glass pots on which no warning encrustation will appear. Paint any damaged areas with Fermate, or other fungicide.

Round-edged plastic and glazed pots are less likely to aggravate this problem than moist, rough clay, or other sharp edges. Many growers put a fold of aluminum foil over clay pot rims, or dip the rims of clean, dry pots ¼ inch deep into a coffee tin of hot paraffin. With this treatment of clay pots, petioles seldom decay. I don't feel, however, that any such artificial arrangement should be necessary. Avoid letting fertilizer salts collect, and you save yourself a lot of trouble.

RING SPOT

Symptoms. Yellow rings of more or less regular outline appear on the upper surfaces of the leaf, as in Figure 39.

Diagnosis. This is ring spot, one of the most easily avoided ailments, although it took considerable research to reveal that it was usually caused by the touching of soil or foliage with water or spray of a temperature varying more than 10 degrees from that of the room in which the saintpaulias were growing. Sunlight on wet foliage also causes ring spot.

Cure and prevention. Use only room-temperature or lukewarm water or spray. When you spray, it is better to have a solution almost hot since it cools considerably in passing through the air. Keep plants away from strong sunlight after showering leaves to free them of dust, or spraying in pursuit of insects.

OTHER PERILS

Bleached leaves. Too much light, too low fertility or lack of trace elements may cause this. Try a chelated fertilizer like Tru-Green.

Brittle leaves. Soil probably lacks magnesium or sulphur or both. Tru-Green is a good chemical source of these trace elements. Rotted leafmold is a good organic addition.

Browned centers. Overfertilizing, a too-rich soil mix, or water settling in crowns may cause this.

Brown spots on leaves. Water getting into the centers of leaves or watering with cold water or chilling of plants may cause this.

Buds but no bloom. Too low humidity or some infestation; raise humidity and spray weekly with an all-purpose insecticide. If no improvement in a month, add dolomite limestone to soil to increase calcium.

Buds dry up. Low humidity, poor air circulation, not enough fresh air, sudden change of environment as when plants are brought from a greenhouse or basement to a window sill, could cause this drying.

Bunched or tight centers. Plants may have been chilled or overexposed to fluorescent lights. Paler-leaved plants in particular are better placed under the ends rather than under the centers of tubes.

Double trouble. When double-flowered varieties do not produce as well as singles, they probably need better light, higher humidity, more plant food (twice as much as singles), and perhaps more water. Covering with plastic at night (plus the above) may stimulate better bloom.

Earthworms. These creatures upset drainage arrangements and disturb roots. Drench the soil with a V-C 13 with chlordane.

Gnarled growth. Treat as for mites.

Leaf stalks soften. Petiole or efflorescence disease attacks at the points where leaf stems touch clay pot rims. Dip the rim in paraffin before planting, or cover with foil. Condition is less likely to occur with plastic pots.

Droopiness on healthy plants. To train leaves back to a proper flat position—it will take a week or so—support them with a cardboard collar. You can make one from a paper plate. Or lay four cardboard strips over the soil to make a square support. Place supports when soil is just a little dry. Then water the plant and mist the foliage immediately, and frequently afterwards.

Long-necked plants. Condition could be the result of poor culture and the reaching of the plant for more light, but it is also common to older plants as a result of the natural loss of lower leaves. To correct: Cut off the plant stalk at the soil line. Remove any older leaves not in first-class condition. Cut the long stalk back according to the depth of the new container, shallow or deep. Place the plant low enough for the crown of leaves to rest just above the soil and pot rim. Wait to fertilize until the stalk has rooted and new growth is apparent.

Powdery mildew. This fungus disease, usually caused by too high humidity or condensation from too great variation of day and night temperatures or cool nights followed by warm days. Spray with Acti-Dione PM every seven to ten days. (In a greenhouse heated by hot water or steam, paint pipes with Fermate or sulfur in winter.)

Root rot. Overwatering is the usual cause. Apply Terraclor or Fermate to soil to check the root-rot fungi.

Rusty brown or bronze stippling on veins of leaves of apparently healthy plants. Probably an infestation of false spider mite brought in from outdoor plants. Dip or spray with Kelthane; be sure to reach underside of leaves. Repeat in seven to ten days as necessary.

Springtails. Narrow white insects, probably harmless, but unsightly, swarming out of drainage holes. Water with a Lindane solution to get rid of them.

QUICK REFERENCE TROUBLE CHART

Use "sterilized" (pasteurized) soil. Segregate new plants for six to eight weeks. Prevent trouble with good culture and an occasional all-purpose insect-fungicide spray. Then you may never have to look below. Preparations mentioned are available at this time but all are subject, of course, to Government control.

What it looks like	What it probably is	Control or cure	Potted plants	Frequency and Remarks
Tiny soft-bodied bugs clustering on tips of growth centers or on buds and flowers, sometimes on roots	Aphids or Plant Lice, green, white, red, brown, purple, white	Malathion 50 or Cythion	1 tsp/1 gal.	7–10 days Avoid exposure to garden flowers.
		Lindane	3 tsp/1 gal.	7–10 days
		NNOR	2 tsp/1 gal.	7–10 days
		Stim-u-plant AV Spray		7–10 days
		Granular systemics		Add to potting soil
Tiny black flies or swarming gnats around plants or crawling over soil	Black Flies, Fungus Gnats. Apparently not harmful except maggot or larvae stage when they attack root hairs	P-40 (AV Miticide)	2½″ potful/ bu. soil	For potting soil only. Aerate well before using.
		Fumi-Soil Capsules	2 caps/1 bu. potting soil	

213

What it looks like	What it probably is	Control or cure	Potted plants	Frequency and Remarks
Gray mold in center, rotting of center leaves	Gray Mold Blight or Botrytis Blight	Zineb 75W	2 tsp/1 gal.	7–10 days. Early diagnosis important. Check for excess humidity, poor ventilation. Discontinue overhead watering.
Plant center turning brown, plant hairs covered with weblike mycelium, center leaves rotting. Leaves droop as when plant needs water. Root system may be disintegrated.	Crown Rot, a fungus often accompanied by root rot, usually caused by overwatering, too high humidity, water running into center of plant.	Phaltan Fermate Terraclor Fumi-Soil Caps	Add 2 tbsp./1 bu. soil Use as dust. Add either to potting mix.	Available 6-oz. can. Dust affected parts and new cuts. Avoid overwatering.

What it looks like	What it probably is	Control or cure	Potted plants	Frequency and Remarks
Leaf cuttings and small plants from seed rot and die.	Damping-off, a fungus disease	Pano Drench	¾ tsp/1 gal.	Drench propagation medium frequently; water cuttings with solution.
Oval insects covered with white mealy wax, cottony masses on petioles and flowers. Plant may appear wilted.	Mealy Bugs, above ground or aerial type	Malathion 50 or Cythion	1 tsp/1gal.	7–10 days preventive spraying
		Alcohol	Paint affected areas with cotton swab.	Wash off leaves after alcohol treatment.
		Prevention: P-40 (AV Miticide) or other granular systemic	2½" potful/ 1 bu. potting soil	Protects up to 6 mos.

What it looks like	What it probably is	Control or cure	Potted plants	Frequency and Remarks
Plant appears wilted. White waxy oval bugs that look like grains of Sponge-Rok usually seen on roots, sometimes on stalk of plant	Soil Mealy Bugs, not bits of Sponge-Rok if they move when prodded	Dr. "V" soil insecticide (aldrin)	4 oz./1 bu. potting soil. For pots: scratch in ¼ tsp. to 3″ pot.	Repeat applications 3 to 6 mos. as required in individual pots or potting soil.
		Cygon 2E Systemic	½ tsp./1 gal. Use as drench.	Apply 7–10 days as required. In severe cases wash soil off roots and dip in drench.
		Isotox Systemic Granules	Mix with potting soil.	

What it looks like	What it probably is	Control or cure	Potted plants	Frequency and Remarks
Leaves in center distorted, brittle, curl up, center tightens, buds and flowers, if any, stunted. Center turns yellow, then gray or brown, finally dies. Then next row of leaves attacked. Pronounced hairiness; off-center desperation growth may appear.	Cyclamen Mites. Minute insects, use magnifying glass. Semi-transparent or glassy.	Contact sprays: Kelthane, Malathion 50, or Cythion	1 tsp/1 gal.	7–10 days. For mites only. General use. Best to alternate brands; mites tend to develop tolerance for one formula.
		Systemic control: P-40 (AV Miticide)	Add 2¼″ potful to 1 bu. soil. Scratch a pinch into soil in each pot.	6 mos. Preventative, not a cure. Safe.
Leaves curl down.	Broad mites, pale almost transparent, move faster than cyclamen mite. Possible infestation by both.	Isotox Systemic (see "Soil Mealy Bugs")		

What it looks like	What it probably is	Control or cure	Potted plants	Frequency and Remarks
Silky cobwebs stretch from leaf to leaf, or cover flowers; leaves gray or reddish-brown, mottled or speckled.	Red Spider Mites. Red, brown, or yellow insects.	Acme or other brand granular systemic		6–8 weeks. Safe. Prevention: (1) Apply a systemic to soil. (2) Regular spraying with contact insecticide. (3) Quarantine newly acquired plants. (4) Isolate plants showing signs of mites.
Stems swollen, especially at base, also leaves. Brown spots sometimes triangular on lower leaves. Center seems to stop growing.	Foliar Nematodes, but same symptoms may indicate other troubles.	P-40 (AV Miticide) or other granular systemic	See "Mites"	Systemic insecticide only way to treat foliar nematodes.

What it looks like	What it probably is	Control or cure	Potted plants	Frequency and Remarks
Plant listless, dwarfed, does not grow, foliage dull and drooping. Roots deteriorated, showing knots and galls.	Root Nematodes	No known cure.		Sterilized potting soil is the only sure control.
Leaf stalks or petioles soggy or jelly-like on plants in clay pots	Petiole Rot or Efflorescence Disease from fertilizer-salt encrustation on pot rims	Phaltan	Dust damaged areas.	Keep fertilizer-salt encrustation off pot rims. Prevention: Dip pot rims in paraffin or cover with foil; or use plastic pots.
Powdery white growth on buds, flowers, flower stems; sometimes on petioles	Powdery Mildew	Acti-Dione PM	2 tbsp/1 gal.	7-day intervals or 3-day if severe. Check ventilation.

What it looks like	What it probably is	Control or cure	Potted plants	Frequency and Remarks
Rings of yellowish splotches or streaks on upper leaf surfaces	Ring spot	Water only with room-temperature water.		Avoid water drops on leaves.
Plant looks wilted but does not respond to watering.	Root Rot	Prevention only: Terraclor or Fermate	Add to potting soil.	Care in watering important. Steam-sterilized soil best precaution.
Soft sluggish insects on bottom of pots or in decaying vegetable matter; holes in leaves	Snails, slugs	Metaldehyde	Dust hiding places.	
Plant wilted or stunted; no growth; does not respond to watering or fertilizer.	Soil pests: earthworms, nematodes, ants, grubs, wireworms, etc.	Fumi-Soil Capsules. Use sterilized soil.	2 caps/1 bu. potting soil	Cover and fumigate soil for 12 days. Effective for 6 mos. Aerate soil 2 weeks before using.

What it looks like	What it probably is	Control or cure	Potted plants	Frequency and Remarks
Tiny white insects dart around in saucers under plants, sometimes on top soil.	Springtails, apparently not harmful as they seem to live on decaying matter in soil.	Lindane soil drench	¼ tsp/1 gal.	Drench soil twice at 7–10-day intervals.
		Malathion 50 spray	1 tsp/1 gal.	Spray every 2–4 weeks.
		V-C 13 with chlordane pot drench	1 tsp/1 gal.	Pot drench good.
Plant does not grow or bloom. If it blooms, blossoms are small, petioles short, leaves in center do not develop.	Stunt Disease. No known remedy, but these symptoms could indicate root damage from symphylids.			Use sterilized soil.

What it looks like	What it probably is	Control or cure	Potted plants	Frequency and Remarks
Plant appears stunted, leaves yellow, root system poor.	Symphylids (garden centipedes)	Lindane	¼ tsp/1 gal.	Soil drench. May require several treatments. Fumi-Soil Capsules, heat sterilization, and Lindane offer prevention methods.
Leaves distorted, wrinkled, or streaked, silver mottling on under side. Blossoms also streaked white and drop prematurely.	Thrips, scrape off green surface with rasping mouth parts.	Malathion 50	1 tsp/1 qt.	Spray 7–10 days, then regularly every 2–4 weeks.
		NNOR	½ tsp/1 qt.	Excellent cure and preventative, or use a systemic.

What it looks like	What it probably is	Control or cure	Potted plants	Frequency and Remarks
Swarms of small white flies congregate on underside of leaves. Leaves speckled or mottled, yellowish or silver. Sometimes a sticky residue on leaves.	Whiteflies	Malathion 50 Lindane NNOR	1 tsp/1 qt. 1 tsp/1 qt. ½ tsp/1 qt.	Spray every 7–10 days, then every 2–4 weeks.
Leaves are mottled green and white and green and yellow; some are spotted or show a mosaic pattern.	Virus Disease			No known remedy. Destroy plants.

THE SAINTPAULIA
LANGUAGE

Acute. Terminating in a sharp point, but not narrow-tapering, said of leaves (or of leaflets, lobes, sepals, petals, bracts, etc.)

Anther. The expanded tip of the stamen. In many flowers—including Saintpaulia—it is borne on a stalk, the filament, and consists of one or more lobes which contain the pollen and open at maturity. In Saintpaulia one can plainly see that the anthers are conjoined—a distinguishing sign of the Gloxinia Family (Gesneriaceae).

Axil. The angle between a branch or leaf and the stem from which it springs. This place in a saintpaulia plant is highly attractive to mealy bugs. In many plants the flower stalks arise from the axils, as in Achimenes and Columnea.

Calyx. The outer and lower series of floral lobes. This external part is usually green—always so in Saintpaulia—in contrast to the inner showy portion or corolla, composed of colored petals.

Capillary attraction. The tendency of a liquid to move into very small interstices in a solid. Thus clay pots or dry soils draw on available moisture nearby. The wick method of watering and watering from the saucer are based on this principle.

Chromosomes. Microscopic bodies, normally definite in number for any given species, in the cells of any living thing, and transmitted through the germ cells of each parent.

Clone or Clon. All of the vegetative offspring of any one plant, arising from cuttings, stolons, suckers, or layering, as distinct from the *seminal* descendants of any plant.

Compost. Organic material readily available to plants for nutriment because it has been thoroughly decomposed by the action of bacteria.

Cordate. Roughly heart-shaped and notched at the base, said of leaves.

Corolla. The unit formed by flower petals. Sometimes the petals are separate, as in the poppy, sometimes united into tubes, and frequently united only at the base or part way, as in Saintpaulia.

Crenate. Edged with scallops or rounded teeth, said of leaves.

Crock. A fragment of a broken clay flowerpot. If you fit a few overlapping pieces together in the bottom of a container to form a drainage area through which water but not soil will pass, you call it "crocking."

Cross-pollination. Transference of pollen from the anthers of a flower on one individual plant to the stigma of a flower on another plant. The plants may be of the same or different varieties, or of the same or different species.

Cultivars. Plants showing variation from the type and which have originated—and are maintained—only in cultivation. Cultivar names are never expressed in Latin, and they should not consist of more than two words. Thus 'Blue Boy' is a cultivar of *Saintpaulia ionantha,* and is set apart by single quotation marks.

Cutting. A piece cut or broken from a parent plant for the purpose of obtaining additional plants of the identical type of the parent.

Dentate. Toothed, said of the margin of a leaf (or of any lobe).

Entire. Smooth-edged, without grooves, scallops, or indentations of any kind, said of leaves (or any lobes).

Flat. A shallow box in which seeds or cuttings are started. The usual size is 16 × 22 inches with a 2- to 4-inch depth. Bottom boards are separated one-quarter inch to permit drainage.

Gene. An unimaginably small molecule or component of a molecule, within the chromosome, bearing permanent, living, and transmissible traits, tendencies, or even modes or rates of operation. Each gene, so far as we know today, involves a single trait or function only.

Genus (plural *genera*). A major subdivision of a plant family, comprising species which are alike in the basic structure of their flowers though differing in other details. Saintpaulia is a genus in the Gloxinia Family (Gesneriaceae).

Germination. The first development of seeds into little plants. The rate of bursting into life depends not only on cultural factors but also on the innate disposition of the variety of the seeds.

Hybrid (L. H. Bailey). "Any product of a cross when the parents were noticeably different from each other, whether the parents belong to different clons, races, or species."

Hydroponics. The science of growing plants in a solution of chemicals and without soil.

Inorganic fertilizer. A manufactured product as nitrate of soda, ammonium sulfate, and muriate of potash.

Medium. The soil, sand, peatmoss, vermiculite, or mixture of any of these, plus other materials, in which seeds are sown, leaves rooted, or plants grown.

Midrib. The central vein of a leaf, which in saintpaulias often appears as a ridgelike extension of the petiole or leaf-stalk.

Mutant (*Variant* or *Sport*). An organism which exhibits transmissible differences from the parent, differences due to changes in the genetic structure brought about by nature, not by hybridization.

Obovate. Inverted ovate; egg-shaped in outline with the narrower end at the base.

Obtuse. Blunt rather than sharply pointed (of leaves or any lobes).

Organic fertilizer. A fertilizer composed of once-living matter, as animal manure, blood, bonemeal, hoof and horn meal; or vegetable residues—grass, leaves, stems, hay, cottonseed meal; or natural mineral products, as ground limestone, phosphate rock, etc.

Ovate. Egg-shaped in outline, with the broader end at the base. (Cf. *cordate,* which is similar but notched at the base.)

Overpot. To use a container too large in relation to the root-earth ball planted in it.

Pedicel. In clusters of flowers, or in panicles or racemes, the stalk that branches from the main stalk to support a single flower and later the seed pod.

Peduncle. The main flower stalk, supporting either a solitary flower or a cluster, spike, or raceme. In Saintpaulia some species bear solitary flowers, on a peduncle, others clusters of flowers, each on its pedicel.

Petiole. The stalk of a leaf.

Pinching. To nip out with thumb and finger the end growth of a branch, or remove tight little buds to make remaining development fuller or to delay flowering.

Pistil. The seed-bearing organ of a flower, consisting of the ovary, the style (where present), and the stigma or stigmas. In some flowers (not Saintpaulia) there is no style.

Plunge. To sink a potted plant up to the rim in soil.

Pollen. The fertile, usually yellow, sperm-bearing grains released from anthers.

Potbound. The condition of a plant whose roots are considerably restricted by the container in which it is growing. If the pot is lifted from such a plant, a mass of roots is revealed, covering the outside of the soil.

Rhombic. Markedly widened through the center, the two sides almost angled, said of leaves or any lobes.

Sepal. A division of the calyx, the usually green cup that surrounds the colored petals. In some flower families the sepals are colored and petal-like, e.g. the Lily Family, the Magnolia Family. Always green in Saintpaulia.

Serrate. Notched or toothed on the edge like a saw.

Shifting. The moving of a plant to the next, larger-sized container with a little more soil but the least possible disturbance. This is in contrast to *repotting* which may involve replacement of wornout soil with a fresh mixture, the improvement of drainage conditions, and even some cutting back of roots. Shifting is for healthy young plants on their way to maturity. Repotting is for established plants in need of reconditioning. In repotting, a larger pot may be provided, the same one used again, or even a smaller one selected, if the previous pot was overlarge.

Sinus. The cleft between two lobes or between the scallops or teeth of a margin.

Species. A group of plants naturally having certain distinctive and constant characteristics, but exhibiting other more basic characteristics in common with other species as subdivisions of a genus. In plant names the first word indicates the genus, the second the species, and the third the variety, as *Saintpaulia ionantha alba.* Instead of variety, the third word may designate a cultivar, as *S. ionantha* 'Blue Boy', but we still popularly call cultivars "varieties."

Sport. Same as *Mutant.*

Stamen. The male reproductive organ of a flower, consisting of a stalk or filament (usually), and a terminal lobe or lobes (the anther) producing and containing pollen. The number and arrangement of stamens vary in different genera, but are essentially the same for all species in any one genus. In Saintpaulia there are two stamens, each having a two-lobed anther, the two anthers touching.

Stigma. That upper part of the pistil which receives the pollen grains and stimulates them to travel as pollen tubes to the ovary to fertilize the egg cells.

Style. A connective, usually stalklike, between the stigma or stigmas and the ovary. It is not present in the flowers of all genera, but quite evident in Saintpaulia.

Sub-irrigation. Watering from the saucer or below the surface of the soil.

Systemic. Pertaining to or affecting the whole organism (plant or animal). A type of insecticide which is absorbed into the sap stream of a plant is called a systemic insecticide or, by usage in horticulture, a systemic.

Variant. Same as *Mutant.*

Variety. A group of plants exhibiting slight modifications (always the same modifications) from the typical and originally described representative of the species.

INFORMATION:
SOCIETIES AND
SOURCES OF SUPPLY

SOCIETIES

If you are interested in growing African-violets and some of the other gesneriads, you will enjoy belonging to one of the societies. All offer helpful cultural leaflets free of charge. To join, simply apply to the society, or fill out the membership application form that you will perhaps find in a friend's copy of a society magazine. Individual, joint, commercial, and associate club memberships are available.

The African Violet Society of America, Inc., AVSA, P. O. Box 1326, Knoxville, Tennessee 37901. Members receive the *African Violet Magazine* and enjoy library facilities and various other privileges. The Society holds a national convention with an African-violet show and judges school every year in a different part of the country.

Saintpaulia International, SI, P. O. Box 10604, Knoxville, Tennessee 37919 publishes the magazine *Gesneriad Saintpaulia News*, GSN, and offers various other benefits to members. A national convention with a saintpaulia and gesneriad show and a judging school is held every year in a different part of the country.

American Gesneriad Society, AGS, 505 South 12th Street, Reading, Pennsylvania 19602. Dues include a subscription to *Gesneriad Saintpaulia News*. The AGS convention and flower show is held with that of SI.

229

American Gloxinia Society, Mrs. Diantha Buell, Eastford, Connecticut 06242. Dues include a subscription to the magazine, *The Gloxinian and the Other Gesneriads.*

Indoor Light Gardening Society of America, Inc., ILGSA, 4 Wildwood Road, Greenville, South Carolina 29607. Dues include a subscription to *The News.*

Interest in the African-violet is by no means limited to the United States. In many far-away lands, there are societies devoted to the plant. Here are three in English-speaking countries:

The African Violet Society of Australia, Mrs. Margaret Thornton, Editor, 60 Guildford Road, Surrey Hills, Victoria, Australia 3127. Individual membership includes a subscription to *News and Views* published in September, December, March, and June.

The African Violet Society of Canada, Mrs. Vera Moir, 45 Highland Avenue, St. Catharines, Ontario. Individual membership includes a subscription to *Chatter,* their quarterly magazine.

Saintpaulia and Houseplant Society, Miss N. Tanburn, Secretary, 82 Rossmore Court, Park Road, London, N.W. 1, England. Membership includes a *Bulletin.* An annual competition is held in late summer in conjunction with one of the Royal Horticultural Society's shows in London.

SOURCES OF SUPPLY

Since growers of fine plants are now legion and their advertisements appear in many publications, I am listing here only the sources of equipment and supplies. Most of the African-violet and gesneriad specialists, such as Fischer's (Linwood, New Jersey) and Tinari's (Huntingdon Valley, Pennsylvania), also offer soil mixtures, fungicides, insecticides, and plant foods, and they carry fluorescent light fixtures, tubes, and timers. These firms specialize in supplies:

Bermas Plastic Co., Inc., Aquamatic Planter Division, Box 534, Bardonia, N.Y. 10954.

Black Magic Products, 421 N. Altadena Drive, Pasadena, Calif. 91107.

Fisher's Quality African Violets, 32 Downsview Ave., Downsview, Ontario, Canada. Blue Whale products; folder free.

Floralite Co., 4124 E. Oakwood Road, Oak Creek, Wis. Fluorescent light equipment; folder free.

Friendly Gardeners, Inc., Box One, Lake Oswego, Ore. 97034. Blue Whale products; folder free.

Bernard D. Greeson, 3548 N. Cramer St., Shorewood, Wis. 53211. Fluorescent light equipment, soil additives, sprays and dusts, supplies in small quantities; list 10¢.

Growers Supply Co., P. O. Box 1132, Ann Arbor, Mich. 48103. Fluorescent light equipment; folder free.

Harborcrest Nurseries, 1425 Benvenuto Ave., Brentwood Bay, Victoria, B. C., Canada. Supplies.

The House Plant Corner, Box 810, Oxford, Md. 21654. Supplies, fluorescent light equipment; catalogue 20¢.

Hydroponic Chemical Co., Inc., Box 97-C, Copley, Ohio 44321. Plant food, insecticides, Wik-Fed pots; catalogue free.

Nature's Way Products, 3505 Mozart Ave., Cincinnati, Ohio 45211. Organic soil conditioners. Send 6¢ stamp for list.

Neas Growers Supplies Co., P. O. Box 8773, Greenville, S. C. 29604. Fluorescent light equipment; 6¢ stamp for list.

George W. Park Seed Co., Inc., Greenwood, S. C. 29646. Supplies, African-violet and other gesneriad seed, including dwarf gloxinias.

Plant Marvel Laboratories, 624 W. 119th Street, Chicago, Ill. 60628. Water-soluble plant foods, aerosol insecticides; supplies; list free.

Shoplite Co., 650 Franklin Ave., Nutley, N. J. 07110. Fluorescent light equipment, accessories, kits, parts; catalogue 10¢.

Stim-u-plant Laboratories, Inc., 2077 Parkwood Ave., Columbus, Ohio 43219. Plant food, insecticides, sprays; catalogue free.

Tube Craft, Inc., 1311 W. 80th Street, Cleveland, Ohio 44102. Fluorescent equipment, trays, timers; catalogue free.

INDEX